PRELUDE TO GLORY

PRELUDE TO GLORY

Wayne D. Leeper

CHRISTIAN COMMUNICATIONS
Nashville, Tennessee

Copyright © 1987 by Gospel Advocate Co.

All rights reserved. No part of this publication may be reproduced, stored in a retrieval system, or transmitted in any form or by any means—electronic, mechanical, photocopy, recording, or any other—except for brief quotations in printed reviews, without the prior permission of the publisher.

Photographs on pages 23, 32, 33, 34, 35, 36, 106 are copyrighted by Holyland Corp., Jerusalem, Israel; the famous model of Jerusalem on the grounds of the Holyland Hotel, Jerusalem. Reprinted by permission.

Photographs on pages 20, 21, 22, 40, 45, 48, 49, 55, 73, 165, 186, 196, 197 are from *"Great people of the Bible and How They Lived."* Copyright © Reader's Digest Assoc. 1974. Reprinted by permission.

The photograph on page 88 is reprinted by permission of Star Bible and Tract Corp.

Christian Communications is a division of the
Gospel Advocate Co., P.O. Box 150, Nashville, TN 37202

ISBN 0-89225-293-6

To Patrice Glyndon Leeper,
my wife and best friend, and
our four beloved children,
Cindy, Stacey, Kevin, and Leslie

Acknowledgment

The author gratefully acknowledges the assistance and cooperation of the many persons and groups who have made this work possible.

A special thanks must go to John and Phyllis Clayton and the staff of *Does God Exist?* in South Bend, Indiana, a nonprofit effort to convince mankind that God is real and the Bible is His word. Without John's encouragement this book would never have been started and without the support and assistance of both John and Phyllis, it would never have been completed.

A special thanks also must go to my friend and teacher, Alex Humphrey, Jr., at Oklahoma Christian College, for his time and effort spent reviewing my manuscript and making valuable suggestions for its improvement.

Mrs. Charlyn Trussell for her many hours spent proofreading and correcting the manuscript.

Dr. Carl Brecheen, Professor of Bible at Abilene Christian University, for reviewing the manuscript.

Mr. Hillel Cherni and the Holyland Corporation and Hotel for allowing me to use pictures of the scale model of *Ancient Jerusalem at the Time of the Second Temple,* constructed on the grounds of the Holyland Hotel in Jerusalem, which enables the reader to visualize life in the city at the time of the second temple, before the Jewish revolt against the Romans and the destruction of the city in A.D. 70. It is constructed according to early and contemporary sources: Josephus, the Mishnah, the Talmud, the

Tosephtha, and the New Testament, as well as recent archaeological discoveries. The model is built to the scale 1:50 (2 cm = 1 m). Insofar as possible, the building materials are the same as were used in the first century B.C.: stone, marble, wood, copper, and iron.

Dorothy M. Harris, Rights and Permissions Supervisor, Reader's Digest Association, Inc., for permission to use pictures from their publication, *Great People of the Bible and How They Lived*, copyright Reader's Digest Association, 1974.

Foreword

Several years ago, I was privileged to sit in a class taught by the author of this book. The study was a harmony study of the life of Jesus from the four Gospels. It became evident to me immediately that Wayne Leeper was the kind of student who did not give up when he found something with difficulty attached to it. In that class, Wayne demonstrated that he had spent much time and effort to find answers to apparent discrepancies. It was also obvious that when he had not found answers, he kept studying until he satisfied his own mind. It was also evident that he did not have a closed mind. He was willing to listen to those in the class, and he appreciated the views of others—even if they did not always agree with his own views.

Since that study with Wayne, I have had the opportunity to study many hours with him, and those early impressions have only been deepened.

It will be obvious to any reader of this book that Wayne has taken some difficult material and tackled it with his presupposition that scripture does not conflict with scripture. He has been tenacious in his research, and when he wasn't satisfied with a particular point, he kept studying until he was satisfied.

He has produced a book that is worthy of anyone's time, and the book will certainly be helpful to those who are in the study of the life of Jesus. It will no doubt become a companion text for college-level studies in the Gospels.

When Wayne started the writing of this book and asked me to

do some reading of the material and some critiquing of it, I was not in agreement with some of his propositions. However, he has done such an excellent work of sustaining what he has affirmed that I find his conclusions difficult to fault.

Wayne Leeper earns his living in secular work, and I am amazed that he has been able to dig so deeply in such a short period of time and come up with the quality found in this book.

I commend the reading of this work by a friend and brother in Christ to any student of Jesus of Nazareth, Son of God and Savior of mankind!

Alex Humphrey Jr.
Oklahoma Christian College
September 30, 1986

***Appendix A*—A History of the Passover** 209
    The Original Passover
    The First Celebration
    Joshua's Passover
    The Feast of Unleavened Bread
    Hezekiah's Passover
    Josiah's Passover
    Ezekiel's Vision
    Ezra's Passover
    Summary of Passover History
    Passover in Jesus' Day
    Conclusion

***Appendix B*—Timetable** 230

***Appendix C*—The Day of Jesus' Crucifixion** 235
    Jewish Sabbath Observances
    The First-day Resurrection
    Three Days and Three Nights
    The Day of Pentecost
    John's High Sabbath
    The Missing Wednesday
    The Day of Preparation
    Conclusion

Bibliography 245

Introduction

Jesus of Nazareth did not live in a vacuum but was very much a part of the history of his day. The picture of his life on earth cannot be fully understood without viewing it against the background of the times in which he lived. This book is a history of the last days of Jesus upon the earth. It begins with his arrival at Jerusalem for the last supper with his disciples and ends with his ascension from the Mount of Olives some forty days later. The majority of the book deals with a period of less than one hundred hours—hours during which the history of the world was radically altered by the actions of one man.

The world does not fully accept the claim that he was the "messiah" of Old Testament prophecy, the Son of God. No one disputes, however, the fact of his existence and the vast effect which that existence has had on the history of the past two thousand years. This book is an attempt to place the man Jesus in his historical setting and in doing so to enhance the reader's understanding of both the man and the times in which he lived. To accomplish this I have compiled several studies into one book.

First, this book is a harmony of Matthew, chapters twenty-six through twenty-eight; Mark, chapters fourteen through sixteen; Luke, chapters twenty-two through twenty-four; and John, chapters thirteen and eighteen through twenty. Every scripture in each of these chapters is used in the harmony. In the cases of parallel passages, I have used the most complete statement and referenced the other passages.

Second, the book is a chronology of the events surrounding Jesus' death, burial, and resurrection. The scriptures have been arranged in such a manner as to present the events of those hours in the sequence in which they occurred.

Third, the book is a historical commentary on the days in which

Jesus lived. Historical comments have been added throughout the book which serve to shed additional light on the events described by the Gospel writers.

Fourth, difficult sections, such as the visits to the tomb and differences between John and the synoptics, have been addressed. My conviction is that there are no contradictions in the scriptures—that the scriptures in their original language are inerrant, divinely inspired, and to be taken literally unless the text or context demands otherwise. Therefore, any seeming contradictions are not without a reasonable and logical explanation and it remains for us to seek and determine that explanation.

Primary Source Material

Three primary sources were used for the material in *Prelude to Glory*.

First, for harmonizing the scriptures, I used the American Standard Version of the Bible. When necessary to go to the Greek to ascertain the exact meaning of a particular word, I used the twenty-first edition of Eberhard Nestle's Novum Testamentum Graece along with Thayer's Greek-English Lexicon. For ease of reading, however, the text as quoted in this book utilizes the wording of the New International Version.

Second, for the study of the development of Judaism and the conditions of Jewish religious life during the last days of the existence of national Israel, prior to its destruction in the first century, my basic source was the Mishnah as translated by Herbert Danby. The Mishnah was written during the second century A.D. and is a codification of the most authoritative Jewish religious regulations of the times.

Finally, for the historical data, I have leaned extensively on the writings of Flavius Josephus as translated by William Whiston. Josephus was a first-century historian of Jewish descent who wrote his history of Israel for the benefit of the Romans. While some of his numbers tend to be exaggerated at times, his insight into the time of Jesus is extremely enlightening.

Additional sources used in this work are included in the Bibliography at the end of the book.

Prelude to Glory

Contents of the Book

The book is comprised of ten chapters, each divided by major and minor headings which make it easy to locate particular discussions. Appendixes have been added to contain in-depth discussions which, if added to the body, would distract from the continuity of the narrative. Chapter One is an overview of first-century Jerusalem intended to give the reader a mental image of the "City of Kings" and Jewish first-century theology. Chapter Two introduces the cast of characters that will be a part of the unfolding drama and includes a discussion of Jesus' Passover celebration. Chapter Three and following contain a harmony and historical narrative.

Limitations of the Book

This book is not intended to be a theological study. Rather, it is a study of the historical events surrounding the death, burial, and resurrection of Jesus of Nazareth. With the exception of a few observations based on these events, no theological applications have been made. That will be left to the student of theology. However, my hope is that the theologian as well as the layman will benefit from the information contained herein.

Insofar as possible, only historical fact has been used in the discussions. When necessary to bring in tradition for purpose of clarification the fact that it is tradition has been emphasized in each instance. Even so, two thousand years have eradicated most of the evidence and even what appears to be factual could contain error.

Finally, this book is neither the beginning nor the end of this particular study. It is but one additional brick added to the body of knowledge of the events surrounding the life of Jesus of Nazareth. It is totally dependent on the many writers who have gone before. None of the information is original although the perspective is perhaps somewhat different. I sincerely believe that others will pick up where this work leaves off and will continue to add to that body of knowledge as we come ever closer to a total understanding of the historical Jesus and the culture in which he lived.

Palestine in Jesus' Day

Prelude to Glory begins with an overview of the "Holy Land" as it existed in Jesus' day. This is the setting in which Jesus' story takes place, and it cannot be understood without first understanding the city and the culture in which he lived. Archaeological discoveries during this century enable us to have an almost perfect picture of Jerusalem as it was when Jesus visited there. The locations of Herod's temple, Herod's palace, the upper room, the Garden of Gethsemane, and the palace of the High Priest are all known locations. The site of the tomb itself is believed to have been narrowed to two possible locations, both of which are open to the public.

Judaism in Jesus' Day

In addition to the city itself, it is necessary also to understand the religious culture in which Jesus lived.

The first five books of the Old Testament were called the Torah. The Torah was the basis of all Jewish religious doctrine, but it was believed and taught by the various rabbinical schools of the day that the Torah must be interpreted in the light of contemporary thought. Thus, the interpretations of the Torah as put forth by the various sages of the day, referred to as the *oral law,* supplemented the teachings of the Torah. It was the combination of the Torah and the oral law that determined Jewish religious practice in Jesus' day. The oral law was so called because, due to the differences between the various schools of thought, no one body of rules was taken to be authoritative, thereby preventing a particular set of rules from being codified in written form. Jewish religious practices in the first century were in a state of constant change and tradition became more important than the written law of God.

Considering this, it is easy to see why the people were astonished when Jesus came teaching "as one who had authority" (Matt. 7:29), and why Jesus would say to the Pharisees and teachers of the law, "You nullify the word of God for the sake of your tradition" (Matt. 15:6).

Therefore, to understand correctly the method of celebrating the Passover in Jesus' day, for instance, one could not go to the

Prelude to Glory

Old Testament but rather had to look to the writings of first-century historians such as Josephus and Pliny.

Purpose of the Book

This study did not begin with any idea that the material would ever be published in book form. Five years ago I was asked to prepare and teach a Bible class on the life of Jesus utilizing all four Gospels. To do this I first prepared a harmony of the four Gospels. Anyone attempting to construct such a harmony is familiar with the problems inherent in such an endeavor.

The most difficult parts of the Gospels to harmonize are those dealing with the death, burial, and resurrection of Christ. His last one hundred hours became a study within itself, and I was intrigued with the events. Determined to do an in-depth analysis of those events, I discovered that the answer to many of the difficulties in harmonizing the Gospels lay in a knowledge of the history and culture of the first century. I later taught a class which dealt with just those one hundred hours, utilizing the harmony, historical data, and visual aids. I have since taught the class to different age groups and different congregations.

For several years friends have been encouraging me to put the material in a form which could be published. Six months ago I agreed to do so and the result is this book. I have mentioned its limitations. Even so, this work is published with the fervent prayer that the knowledge contained herein will be of benefit in the furthering of His kingdom.

Jesus did many other miraculous signs in the presence of his disciples, which are not recorded in this book. But these are written that you may believe that Jesus is the Christ, the Son of God, and that by believing you may have life in his name.

John 20:30–31

CHAPTER ONE

Palestine in Jesus' Day

Jerusalem, in Jesus' day, was an occupied city striving to maintain its national existence under the combined oppression of Roman rule and Hellenizing influences.

History: the Beginning of the End

The end for national Israel began with the carrying away into captivity of the northern kingdom by the Assyrians and, finally, the Babylonian captivity of the southern kingdom. When, in 536 B.C., the Jews in Babylon were allowed to return to the "Land" only three of the original twelve tribes made the journey. These three returned to find the Samaritans in control of the central portion of what had been the nation of Israel. Only in Galilee in the north and Judea in the south did they make the attempt to restore Mosaic Judaism.

Jerusalem itself was in such a dilapidated condition that years were required just to make the basic repairs. Years more would pass before the city was fully restored. While it would be physically restored and even enhanced far beyond what it had been in the days of David and Solomon, it would never again enjoy the level of spiritual morality achieved in earlier years. The city would continue to exist until A.D. 70 but always in a state of gradual moral decline. The last of the Old Testament prophets had been dead for more than four hundred years by the time Jesus was born, and the absence of their influence became more obvious with every year that passed.

Alexander the Great

In 325 B.C. Alexander the Great made the entire Middle East and Northern Africa a part of his Grecian Empire. With him came

JERUSALEM AT THE TIME OF THE CRUCIFIXION

Legend

A. Temple
B. Court of Gentiles
C. Fortress Antonia
D. Hippodrome
E. Theater
F. Viaduct
G. Herod's Palace
H. Mount of Olives
I. Kidron Valley
J. Palace of High Priest
K. Garden of Gethsemane
L. Golgotha
M. Upper Room
N. Garden Tomb

Palestine in Jesus' Day

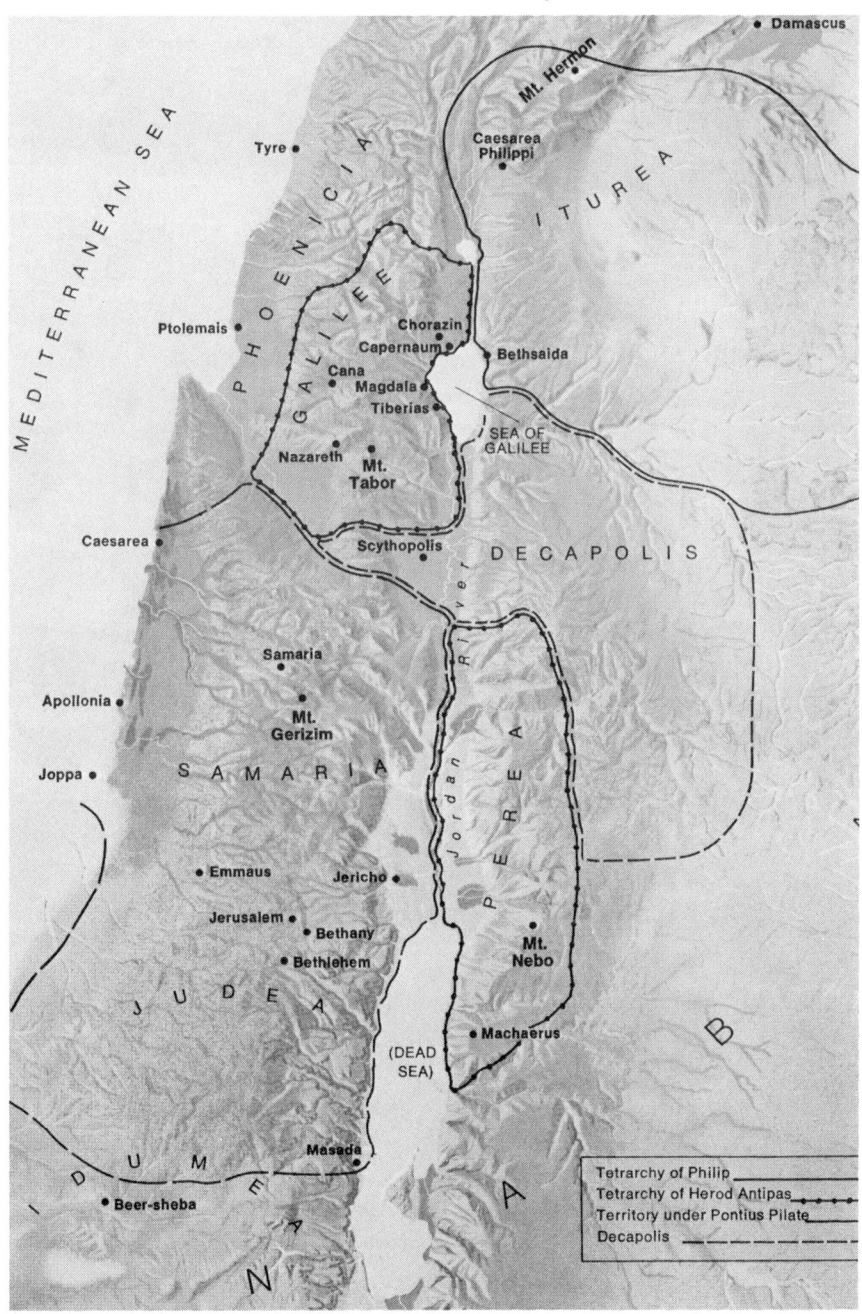

Map of Palestine in Jesus' time

Prelude to Glory

The Greeks: Bearers of a New Culture

Roman Legions

the Greek, or Hellenizing, influences which gradually replaced the ancient Jewish standards of morality. Intermarriage became more commonplace. Greek theatre, art, architecture, and culture gradually began to influence the way of life in Jerusalem. The resistance to this was strong but like a gradually rising tide it could not be kept from eroding the sands of Mosaic Judaism. By Jesus' time the ancient language of Hebrew was to be found only in the worship service. Like Latin today, it had been replaced as both the language of the common man and the language of officialdom. The common man now spoke Aramaic and those who had enough education to write did so in koine Greek. Greek was the language used in all official documents and written correspondence. It was the language of commerce, drama, and literature. The tide of change would not be stopped.

The Romans

In 63 B.C. Roman legions under the command of Pompey marched into Jerusalem, thus completing their conquest of the land of Palestine and putting an end to the civil war that had been

Prelude to Glory

ravaging the country for four years. With the Romans came another way of life which would further undermine the national existence and the ancient religion of the Jews. Whereas the Greeks had emphasized culture and education, the Roman standard of achievement was always that of power.

Influential families would be enticed to accept and support the Roman presence through offers of Roman citizenship. This is believed to have been the way the apostle Paul's family gained its Roman citizenship. Wealthy families, such as the Herods, would send their sons to Rome to be trained and educated. The "upper city" of Jerusalem was occupied by the privileged class comprised of both Jews and Romans.

Tiberius Caesar

The entire religious system that had been ordained of God and known as the Law of Moses had been fragmented into numerous sects based on "the traditions of men." Each sect was in its own way striving to maintain acceptance in the eyes of God while bending as necessary to accommodate the system under which it existed. The Pharisees looked to their piety; the Sadducees, their conservatism; the Essenes, their seclusion; and the Scribes, their knowledge of the law. The Zealots, learning from the Romans, looked to the sword as the means by which to preserve their national existence, while at the same time holding themselves out to be a religious sect. Under this guise, religion was practiced more as a means of national preservation than as worship of God.

Rumors of the arrival of a messiah found fertile ground in many a heart as the means by which the Roman yoke of oppression would be cast off. His coming was looked to, not as a means of salvation for the spirit, but rather for the establishment of a kingdom like that of their father David and the restoration of national independence.

The outward ordinances of the temple worship were faithfully maintained while the soul of the nation slowly died. The religious offices, once reserved for the righteous, now became rewards for faithful service to Rome. Only in the small rural villages of Galilee and Judea could one occasionally find righteous men and godly hearts still striving to serve faithfully him who lives forever.

Government

Herod the Great. In 37 B.C. Herod became king of all Judea. Herod was an Idumean and his appointment as king resulted in a brief revolt by the Hasmoneans who objected to the children of Jacob being ruled by a descendant of Esau. Herod was forced to flee to his fortress at Masada, near the Dead Sea, from which he managed to get to Rome. Mark Anthony proceeded to resubdue the province so that Herod could establish his rule. He became known as "Herod the Great" and is the Herod associated with the slaughter of the babies at Bethlehem some thirty-five years later. In order to gain acceptance with the Jews, Herod ordered the rebuilding of the temple which began in 20 B.C., and in an effort to bring Roman culture to this eastern province he initiated a number of other civic improvements which will be discussed later in this chapter. Herod the Great had seven sons, three of whom would receive a portion of his kingdom and become figures in the New Testament.

Herod Antipas. Herod Antipas was the Herod who presided over one of Jesus' trials. He was reared and educated in Rome. At his father's death he received the provinces of Galilee and Perea. He built the city of Tiberias, on the shore of the Sea of Galilee, to serve as his capital. It was there that he dwelt the greater part of the time, going to Jerusalem only for feast days and other important events. He formed an unholy attachment for Herodias, wife of his brother Philip. (This is another brother, not Philip the Tetrarch mentioned in the Gospels.) The condemnation by John the Baptist of his subsequent marriage to Herodias resulted in Herod's having John executed. Herod was later banished to Spain by the Roman government and remained there until his death.

Herod the Tetrarch. Herod the Tetrarch received the area above Perea which included Iturea, Trachonitus, Gaulanitis, Auranitis, and Batanea. His rule was characterized by justice and modera-

Prelude to Glory

Herodium

HEROD THE GREAT
King over all Palestine
37 B.C. - 4 B.C.

ARCHELAUS
Ethnarch of Judea, Samaria & Idumea
4 B.C. - A.D. 6

Replaced by Roman Procurators - A.D. 6
1. Coponius   A.D. 6 - A.D. 10
2. M. Ambivius   A.D. 10 - A.D. 13
3. Annius Rofus   A.D. 13- A.D. 15
4. Valerius Gratus A.D. 15 - A.D. 26
5. PONTIUS PILATE   A.D. 26 - A.D. 36

HEROD PHILIP
Tetrarch of Iturea, Trachonitus,
Gaulanitis, Auranitis, & Batanea
4 B.C. - A.D. 34

HEROD ANTIPAS
Tetrarch of Galilee & Perea
4 B.C. - A.D. 39

BIBLE REFERENCES

Herod the Great   -   Matt. 2: 1-19
                  -   Luke 1: 5
Archelaus   -   Matt. 2: 22
Herod Philip   -   Luke 3: 1
Herod Antipas   -   Mark 6: 14-29
                  -   Luke 3: 1; 13: 31-35
                           23: 7-12
Pontius Pilate   -   Matt. 27: 2ff
                  -   Mark 15: 1ff
                  -   Luke 23: 1ff
                  -   John 18: 29ff

Diagram—Political Structure of Palestine in Jesus' Day

27

Prelude to Glory

Tiberias—Herod's Capital City

tion. Jesus would sometimes go to this region to find peace and rest. Herod later married Salome, the daughter of Herodias and Philip, the same Salome who had previously asked for the head of John the Baptist. He ruled until his death in A.D. 34.

Archelaus. Archelaus, who like Antipas was reared in Rome, became Ethnarch of Judea, Samaria, and Idumea. He used his father's palace in Jerusalem as his capital. It was the news of Archelaus' ascent to the throne which caused Mary and Joseph to bypass Judea and make their home in Nazareth of Galilee. He was the worst of Herod's sons and his rule became so cruel that in A.D. 6 he was banished to Vienna by the Emperor Augustus in order to prevent a revolt by the people. Following that, the provinces of Judea, Samaria, and Idumea were placed under the rule of Roman procurators.

Palestine in Jesus' Day

The Roman Procurators. The Roman procurators ruled Judea, Samaria, and Idumea until the destruction of Jerusalem in A.D. 70. The procurator who ruled from A.D. 26 to A.D. 36 was a Roman by the name of Pontius Pilate. When Pilate was appointed procurator by Tiberius, he selected the city of Caesarea on the Mediterranean Sea as his capital. He was the fifth procurator of the area and would figure prominently in the trial and crucifixion of Jesus. Pilate was dismissed from his position, and tradition says that he died by suicide.

Jerusalem

Jerusalem was built on three hills. The central and tallest of the three was Mount Moriah where two thousand years earlier Abraham had brought Isaac to be offered as a sacrifice. The Jebusites subsequently settled on the hill and built a fortified city, which David selected as his capital when he became King of Israel. Solomon chose the top of the mount as the site for his famous temple, but in Jesus' day Herod's temple dominated the summit. The old "City of David," referred to as the "lower city," occupied the southern slope, and just across the south wall lay the Valley of Gehenna.

At the base of the west slope of Mount Moriah was the Tyropean Valley which separated Mount Moriah from Mount Zion. Herod built his Palace on Mount Zion and around it grew up what became known in Jesus' time as the new or "upper" city.

To the west of Mount Moriah was the valley of the Kidron. A small brook ran through the Kidron Valley, which separated Mount Moriah from the third of the three hills, the Mount of Olives, so-called because of the many olive groves that covered its slopes. Beyond the Mount of Olives, about two miles from Jerusalem, was the small village of Bethany. About halfway up the Mount of Olives a merchant had built an olive press to process the olive oil which was the city's leading export. Behind the press was a garden, known as the "Garden of the Olive Press." In Aramaic it was the Garden of Gethsemane.

Prelude to Glory

Restoration by Herod the Great

Between 37 B.C. and 4 B.C., Herod transformed the city as had no other ruler since Solomon. There were basically two reasons for this. One was to gain acceptance among the people of Palestine. The second, and perhaps more important in Herod's mind, was to increase his capital's importance on the political and cultural map of the Roman Empire. In addition to the restoration of the temple, Herod's improvements included palaces, a citadel, a theater, a hippodrome, viaducts, and public monuments. What had originally been a Maccabean fortress adjacent to the temple was rebuilt on a grand scale and renamed Antonia, after his friend Mark Antony.

The City that Jesus Entered

No visitor seeing Jerusalem for the first time could fail to be impressed by its visual splendor. As a traveler rounded the Mount of Olives on the road from Bethany, he saw the city in full view across the Kidron Valley. The scene from the Mount of Olives was dominated by the gleaming, gold-embellished temple, the most hallowed spot in the Jewish world. This was the Lord's earthly dwelling place, the focal point of the Jews' most solemn rites and celebrations. It stood high above the old City of David at the center of a gigantic white stone platform. South of the temple was the lower city—built by the Jebusites—a sea of limestone houses, buff-colored from years of sun and wind, amid narrow unpaved streets. The upper city—built by Herod—was marked by white marble villas and palaces of the very rich. Two large, arched passageways, or viaducts, spanned the Tyropean Valley which separated the lower city from the upper city (Zion). These allowed the wealthy to travel from their homes to the temple without passing through the masses of people occupying the lower city.

A high, thick, stone wall encircled Jerusalem. In Jesus' day this wall was approximately three and a half miles in circumference and enclosed an area of slightly less than one square mile. At intervals along the wall were gates with custom stations and publicans collecting taxes on goods entering and leaving the city. Much of the controversy surrounding the location of the

Palestine in Jesus' Day

Jerusalem—Model of City in Jesus' Day

crucifixion and burial of Jesus centers on the exact location of the "second" wall. The first wall was built by the Jebusites and surrounded only the lower city. The second wall was built later to accommodate the expanding population.

The Lower City

The lower city occupied an area of approximately 215 acres, about half of which was occupied by the temple and other religious buildings, leaving a little more than 100 acres to accommodate the forty to fifty thousand people believed to occupy it at that time. This works out to a population density of approximately 450 people per acre. A traveler arriving from Bethany would enter the "lower city" part of Jerusalem through a gate at the north end of the eastern wall, just south of where it joined the temple. This is the gate through which Jesus made his triumphal entry into the city (John 12:12–13), and through which he again entered the city when he arrived to celebrate the

Prelude to Glory

Houses in the Lower City

Passover with his disciples. This was also the gate which led to the Mount of Olives.

Just inside the gate was a maze of dusty streets and alleyways where the traveler's senses would immediately be assaulted by dust and heat, the sound of voices raised in anger or song, the clatter of hooves, and the odors of cooking food. The "Small Market Street" in the lower city contained open-air shops where Jerusalem's craftsmen sat at work—weavers, potters, bakers, tailors, carpenters, and metal workers. Closer to the temple was the market where merchants sold fruits and vegetables, dried fish, sacrificial animals, clothes, perfumes, and jewelry. The market street was always crowded and busy, especially on Mondays and Thursdays, the main market days. Only on the Sabbath was the street empty and quiet. The traveler could stop and rest at one of the many taverns or restaurants. Food included fresh or salted fish, fried locusts, vegetables, soup, pastry, and fruit. For a beverage he had his choice of local wine or imported beer.

Palestine in Jesus' Day

Herod's Palace

Occupations ranged from craftsman to farmer. Farmers of Jerusalem, like their rural cousins, went outside the city each morning to tend the crops. Most of them worked in the rich olive groves that covered the surrounding hillsides and provided the city's only major export. The city's numerous craftsmen were organized into guilds. The members of each particular guild lived in a cluster of houses in a particular section of the city and worked in communal shops. In most cases, each guild had its own synagogue of which there were at least 480 in Jerusalem at the time of Christ. Most of Jerusalem's working people lived in the crowded, noisy precincts of the lower city.

The Upper City

In contrast to the lower city, the broad fashionable avenues of the upper city were laid out in an orderly grid pattern like the

Prelude to Glory

The Agora in the Upper City

stately city of Rome. This part of Jerusalem was the home of the rich and powerful Jewish families and high-ranking Roman officials. They lived in spacious white marble mansions and palaces built around courtyards with formal gardens and pools. These people traveled by chariot or carriage and were waited on from morning to night by an array of various servants. It was in this part of the city that Jesus is believed to have used one of the large upper rooms for the last meal with his disciples.

The royal palace of Herod the Great was situated in the upper northwest corner of this section of Jerusalem. This palace would later be used by his sons when visiting Jerusalem from their respective capitals and is where Jesus was brought before Herod on the morning of his crucifixion.

Directly in front of the palace stood the upper market, Agora. It had Roman-style arcades along three sides and an open court for market booths in the center. Here were the shops of the dealers in luxury goods, the distillers of expensive oils and perfumes, the master tailors and silk merchants, the goldsmiths and silver-smiths, the dealers in ivory and incense and precious stones. Here the rich and noble of Jerusalem would do their shopping and pass away the time visiting with friends. Not far away was the palace of the Jewish high priest. It was to this palace that Jesus was brought following his arrest and where Peter's denials took place. The high priest at the time of Jesus' trial was Caiaphas, the son-in-law of Annas.

Herod's Theatre

The Hippodrome

The Temple

Herod the Great had also built a theater in the upper city. Here on warm nights the classical Greek tragedies would be acted out for the entertainment of the wealthy. It was a large open-air auditorium with semicircular seating ascending from a central stage. Wealthy Jews came here along with the Romans to watch the best of Greek and Roman drama. Most traditional Jews, however, scorned this and other outgrowths of Greek-Roman culture as immoral.

On the eastern side of the upper city was the hippodrome, a large open-air arena where the sporting events took place. Chariot racing and the gladiatorial events were among the favorites. Olympian type contests were also held in this arena.

The most dominant structure in the city of Jerusalem was the great Temple of Herod, which he had erected on the site of the original Temple of Solomon. This was his great gift to the Jewish nation.

Herod's Temple

Directly across the Tyropean Valley from the upper city, in the northeastern corner of Jerusalem, stood the incomparable temple, the city's crowning jewel. Built by Herod as a goodwill gesture toward his hostile Jewish subjects, it was reputedly one of the finest religious structures in the world. The central sanctuary was approached through a series of outer courts, each court becoming progressively more exclusive.

TEMPLE MOUNT

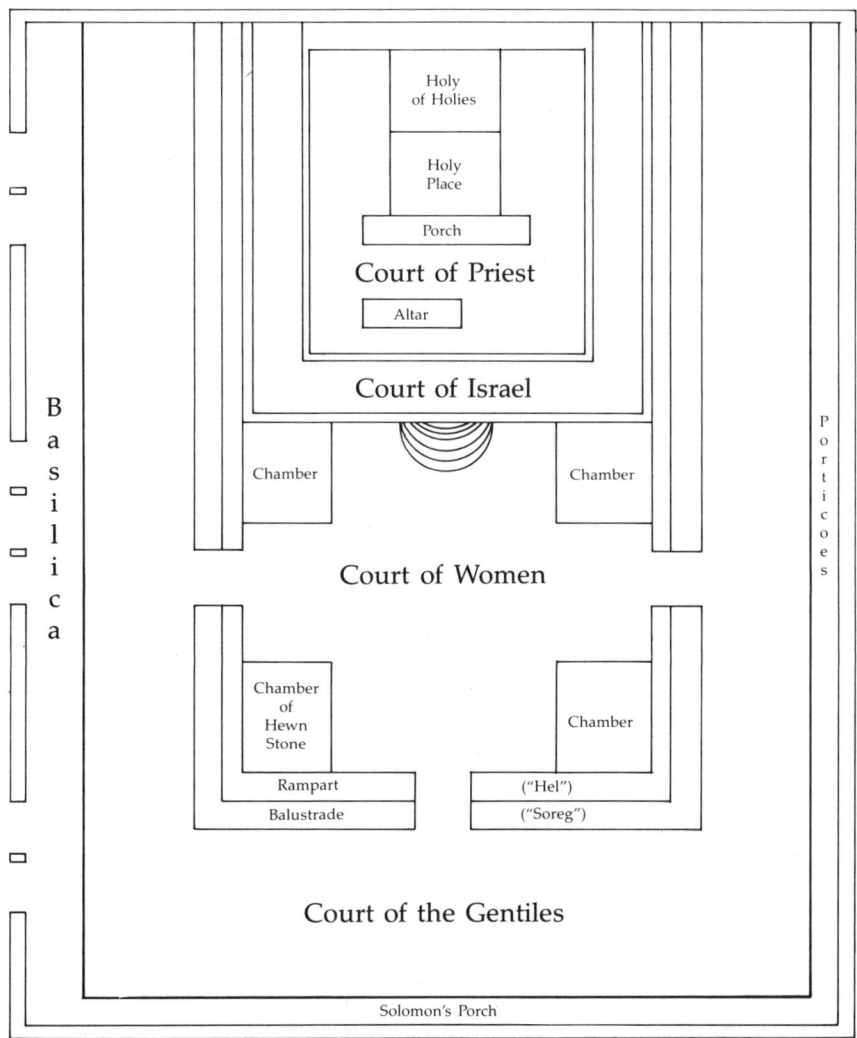

Diagram—Interior Arrangement of Temple

Prelude to Glory

The Court of the Gentiles. This court was the outermost court and was comprised of a huge rectangular area of about thirty-five acres. It was paved with colored stones and enclosed by tall stately columns. Visitors entered through immense double and triple gates, which were open to gentiles as well as Jews. At the center stood a second enclosed compound posted with signs in Greek and Latin, warning:

> No foreigner is allowed within the balustrades and embankment about the sanctuary. Whoever is caught will be personally responsible for his ensuing death.

Only Jewish men and women could venture beyond this point, which led through three large gates into the Court of Women.

The Court of Women. This court was also surrounded with ornate columns. On its western side was a curved flight of fifteen stairs which rose to the Nicanor Gate. Beyond the gate lay the Court of Israel. Women were not permitted beyond the Court of Women; however, they were allowed to ascend to a balcony to look over the wall and observe what was taking place within the Court of Israel.

The Court of Israel. The Court of Israel was a long narrow area surrounding the Court of the Priest. Only priests were allowed beyond this point. It was to this court that the men would bring their animals to be sacrificed. Only a low balustrade separated this area from the Court of the Priest.

The Court of the Priest. This area was accessible only to the priests and Levites who served in the temple. In the center of this area was the great horned altar of sacrifice with a long ramp leading to the top. It was upon this altar that the blood would be poured and the fat burned when the Passover lamb was brought to be sacrificed. Dominating the entire complex was the majestic sanctuary which stood at the west end of the Court of the Priests.

The Sanctuary. The sanctuary was built of perfectly tooled and pitted white marble stones that were covered with plates of heavy gold. Golden spikes rose from the roof which soared to a height of about 165 feet. At the back of a large porch were vast gilded doors covered by a Babylonian tapestry of blue, purple, crimson, and gold, depicting the heavens. Above the porch was a golden vine, the symbol of the nation of Israel. It was said that there was so much gold covering the building that no one could look directly at it in bright sunlight. Inside the sanctuary were two rooms: the Holy Place and the Holy of Holies.

The Holy Place. The Holy Place was a large hall paneled in cedar. It contained a golden altar for incense, a golden table for the bread offering, and a golden seven-branched candelabrum lit by seven lamps burning pure olive oil. Separating the Holy Place from the Holy of Holies was a sixty-foot veil of pure spun gold which ran from the ceiling to the floor.

The Holy of Holies. Only the high priest was allowed to enter the Holy of Holies and then only on the Day of Atonement which was once every year. Within this chamber, believed to be the actual dwelling place of God on earth, was absolutely nothing. The Ark of the Covenant had once occupied the Holy of Holies, but by the time of Jesus it had been destroyed. The absence of objects from the Holy of Holies in Jesus' day was said to symbolize the intangible and invisible presence of God.

Construction of the Temple

Building the temple required the services of more than ten thousand laborers. Herod had one thousand priests especially trained as carpenters and masons to work on the sanctuary, for, by law, no layman was allowed to handle the sacred building materials. The sanctuary was completed in eighteen months but the outer courtyards were not completed until A.D. 64, only six years before its destruction by the Roman armies. During this entire time the temple ritual was never interrupted.

The Fortress of Antonia

Along the northern side of the temple courtyard stood the massive palace-fortress of Antonia. A stairway and an under-

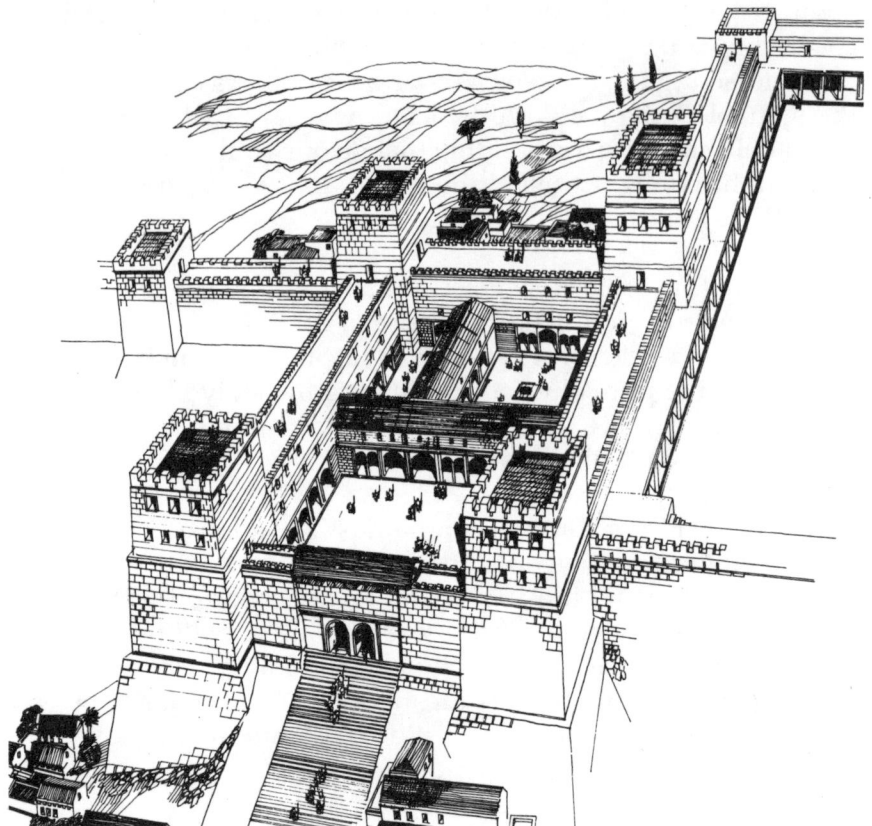

Fortress of Antonia where Jesus was Scourged

ground passageway connected Antonia with the Court of the Gentiles. The six hundred Roman soldiers stationed there were always on the alert for disturbances in the temple precincts. Realizing the power of the high priest's office, the Romans had taken custody of the priest's ceremonial robes and kept them in one of Antonia's four guard towers, releasing them only on important religious feast days. They sought to limit the priest's power by restricting the use of the robes, which symbolized his authority. In the century before the Roman occupation in 63 B.C., the king of Israel had also been the high priest and both offices had been hereditary. The Romans abolished the kingship and made the office of the high priest appointive. Nevertheless, in Jesus' day, the high priest remained the most powerful figure in the Jewish nation. It was to this fortress that Jesus was taken for his trials before Pilate. It was here also that Judas came to obtain the soldiers who helped him in the arrest of Jesus.

The Priesthood

The High Priest

The office of high priest carried with it a number of unique privileges and responsibilities. Under Roman rule this office became one of political patronage. Annas, one of the high priests at the time of Jesus, was so powerful and influential with the Romans that he was able to have not only himself but five of his sons plus a son-in-law and a grandson, Jonathan, appointed to the position and thus established a dynasty which lasted for years. As head of the Sanhedrin or Jewish high court, the high priest presided over the nation's highest administrative and judicial body. His daily life was governed by the strictest rules of ceremonial purity. Even after retiring from office he continued to wield great influence. Thus, Annas was the man to whom Pilate directed that Jesus be taken following his arrest.

The Chief Priests

The high priest stood at the apex of an elaborate hierarchy of temple personnel, just above the chief priests. The chief priests numbered two hundred and were selected from among the prominent families of Israel. As benefactors of the prestige that came with being held in high esteem by the Romans, they had perhaps the most to lose should the system be overthrown. This probably accounts for much if not all of their animosity toward Jesus. The most important of these men was the Captain of the Temple. He was second only to the high priest in both rank and power. His duties included supervision of the whole body of priests and of all temple activities. The other chief priests had charge of the daily and weekly temple services, the temple treasury, and the maintenance of the sacred vessels.

Priests of the Temple

Below the chief priests were the ordinary priests of the temple. There were about seventy-two hundred of them in Jesus' time. These were men who could trace their descent back to Aaron and are commonly referred to as the Aaronic priesthood. Most of them lived outside of Jerusalem in the villages of Galilee and Judea. They were divided into twenty-four priestly clans, each of which served a week at a time in the temple. Their duties included lighting the altar fires, attending to the offerings of incense and unleavened bread, and the killing of the sacrificial animals.

The Levites

The lowest ranking temple officials were the Levites. These descendants of Levi are referred to as the Levitical priesthood. There were some ninety-six hundred Levites in the first century, and they were also divided into twenty-four clans, each serving a week at a time in the temple. The Levites served as guards, policemen, doorkeepers, singers, musicians, and servants of the temple. They were forbidden, on pain of death, to enter the holy sanctuary or to approach the altar of sacrifice.

The Temple Ritual

The daily temple ritual required the services of nearly one thousand chief priests, priests, and Levites. On feast days such as the Passover, all twenty-four clans of the Aaronic and Levitical priests were required to come to Jerusalem to participate in the elaborate ceremonies and sacrificial rites. This meant that there were nearly seventeen thousand temple personnel on hand during each of the three great pilgrim festivals.

Pilgrim Festivals

During the festival weeks, the population of Jerusalem was increased from approximately fifty thousand to more than one hundred thousand. The pilgrims' presence provided an important stimulus to the city's economy. Besides creating a huge demand for food, lodging, and sacrificial animals, the incoming pilgrims were required to spend a tenth of their annual income, after taxes, within Jerusalem. This was in addition to the "tithe" they had to pay directly to the temple.

Many pilgrims found lodging in one of Jerusalem's inns or private homes. Some of the foreign Jewish communities had built hospices for their citizens to use when they visited the Holy City. The Essenes and Pharisees also provided lodging for their fellow members. The vast majority, however, stayed in tents outside the city walls or in the villages of Bethphage and Bethany, as did Jesus and his disciples. The overcrowding and the excitement of the festivals frequently led to outbreaks of violence and anti-Roman riots. On more than one occasion the huge mass of pilgrims was stirred up by zealous nationalists or would-be messiahs. For this reason, the Roman governor made a point of being present during these occasions, and extra soldiers were stationed at strategic locations throughout the city.

Religious Sects

The supreme ruling body of the Jewish nation at the time of Jesus was the Sanhedrin. It was comprised of seventy-one members selected from the chief priests, elders, and scribes. The high priest served as the presiding officer. Although in theory the Sanhedrin had executive and legislative functions as well as judicial authority, its power was reduced considerably by the Roman rulers. Its decisions were subject to review by the Roman authorities and it was not allowed to impose and carry out the death sentence. Its members came primarily from the wealthy upper class of Jewish citizens.

High Priests and Chief Priests

The high priests and chief priests formed an elite religious nobility within Jerusalem. Members were selected from a small number of wealthy families who traced their descent back to Zadok, the high priest during Solomon's reign. These men controlled not only the temple but a large number of seats on the Sanhedrin.

Elders

These were an influential lay-nobility within Jerusalem, represented by members who sat on the Sanhedrin. They were descendants of ancient ruling families whose power had originated in the days following the conquest. Many of the elders were wealthy merchants and landowners. Elderships had originally been established by Moses in each city to serve as judges (Ex. 18:17–23). Through the centuries, however, they became positions of power and prestige.

Sadducees

The priests and elders made up a party known as the Sadducees, which was formed about 200 B.C. as the party of the high priest and aristocratic families. They controlled the temple and the affairs of the country as representatives of the priestly aristocracy supporting the Hasmonean rulers. Even under Roman rule, through the Sanhedrin in which many were members, they exercised considerable political control over the people of Palestine. They were more apt to adopt Hellenism and were in favor with the Roman authorities. They had a more anthropomorphic view of God than did the Pharisees and rejected divine providence because they did not consider God to be interested in human affairs. As the conservative element in Jewish religion, they rejected the oral law and accepted only the written law of Moses. The Sadducees denied the resurrection of the body, the existence of angels and emphasized the sacrificial cult of the temple. Since they were a political group and considerably opposed to Christian doctrine, the church had more to fear from them than some of the other Jewish sects.

Scribes

In the decades just before and during the time of Jesus, the dominant role of the Sadducean families was being overtaken by a new dynamic ruling class called scribes. These men came from all classes—priests, merchants, artisans, and laborers—and their authority rested on their learning. Anyone could become a scribe, but those choosing to do so had to devote years of study to that end. They were required to master the law and scriptures by the age of fourteen. Thereafter, they had to spend years associated with recognized teachers who gave them lengthy instruction in personal conduct and the application of the law in everyday situations. Such teachers were so venerated that pupils often observed not only their teachings but their actions as well. When a student reached a point where he could make his own decisions on points of law and justice, he became a nonordained scholar. Only at about the age of forty would he be formally ordained as a scribe in his own right, and from that time on he could be addressed as rabbi. The scribes were held in great awe and respect throughout the Jewish world and could be recognized on the streets by their long, flowing robes, fringed at the corners with very long tassels. When a scribe passed, ordinary people rose as a sign of respect. They were given the place of honor at important feasts and in the synagogues.

A Pharisee Shows Religious Zeal

Pharisees

The Pharisees were a group of laymen who chose to live in strict adherence to scribal tradition and law. Although some were scribes, the majority were simple, uneducated men. It was their extreme piety rather than their wisdom that set them apart and they often went to great lengths to demonstrate that piety. They lived in communities and membership was limited to men who had shown their ability to follow a stringent set of rules. Arising from the mass of people, the Pharisees waged a vigorous struggle to remove Jewish religion from the control of the priests. They removed several ceremonies from the temple and placed them in the Jewish home.

While the Sadducees occupied themselves with the temple, the Pharisees proclaimed to the people the law of God. They were more liberal and flexible in interpreting the law of God than were the Sadducees. They believed God to be omnipotent—all-wise, all-knowing, and all-present. They believed that God had created in man two impulses, one to do evil and the other to do good, and that man had the free will to choose between them. The Torah, which consisted of the first five books of the Old Testament, was to be interpreted with God-given reason in view of the ideas and knowledge of each age. True worship was not sacrifice but the study of the Torah. They believed God to be in total control, helping people. Probably New Testament references against the Pharisees were against the insincere ones, who were condemned by even their followers. Jesus referred to some of these as hypocrites and vipers; Paul, however, was proud of his heritage as a Pharisee. Pharisaic beliefs were in keeping with much of early Christian theology.

Herodians

This group arose during the time of the Herodian dynasty. They supported Herod and the Herodian dynasty and accepted Hellenization and foreign rule. They were from the wealthy class of Idumeans and had great political influence. The Herodians were more of a political group than a religious one. They hoped to preserve national existence through a policy of accommodation with the Romans. Although they were directly antagonistic toward the Pharisees, they united with them in their opposition to Jesus.

Zealots

This was a band of Jewish freedom fighters who hated Romans and Roman rule. Their primary goal was the liberation of Palestine from under the yoke of Rome. They were active from about 37 B.C. to A.D. 70 and would not tolerate peace with idolatrous Rome. As fanatics for the Jewish faith and the Torah, their religious zeal gave them their name, and they refused to pay taxes and terrorized their political opponents and Roman rulers. The apostle Simon

Masada—General View with Roman Camps

Excavations at Qumran

Prelude to Glory

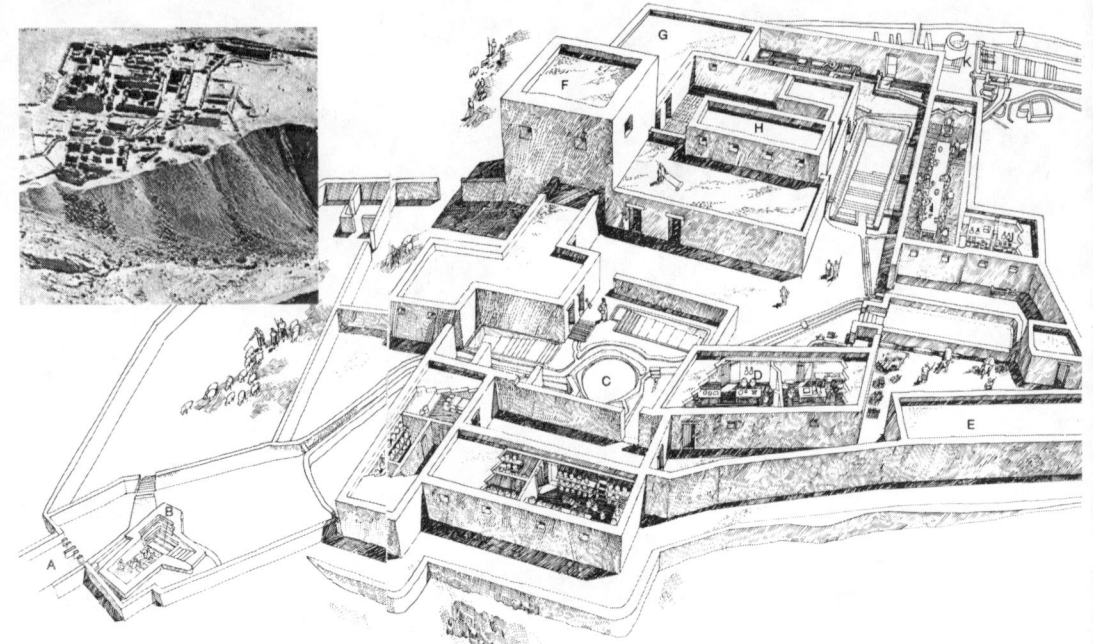

The Essene Community at Qumran

had been a Zealot and some sources claim that Peter had been also. Barabbas, the man released in the place of Jesus, was a leader among the Zealots. A subgroup within the Zealots was known as the Sicarii, which means "daggermen." Between A.D. 50 and A.D. 70 bands of these Sicarii assassins plundered and terrified Judea. They were leaders in the final rebellion that brought about the destruction of Jerusalem and were the group who made their last stand at Masada.

Essenes

Both Josephus and Pliny mention the Essenes in their writings, but until very recently little has been known about them. Qumran, the religious community where the Dead Sea Scrolls were discovered, is now considered to have been an Essenes community. This sect of the Jews, active between 110 B.C. and 70 A.D., practiced a strict ceremonial asceticism, discouraging marriage and promoting community ownership of goods. They were known to be temperate, industrious, charitable, and opposed to all oaths, to slavery, and to war. Shrinking from communion with other worshippers whose contact they regarded as defilement, they avoided the temple and sacrificed in their own dwellings. Engedi, on the western shores of the Dead Sea, and other solitary places were their favorite haunts. They adhered strictly to the law of Moses and rejected all oral law. Accordingly, they celebrated the Passover within the family context on the fourteenth of Nisan in keeping with the ancient commandments rather than accepting the change to the fifteenth as was then the practice of national Israel. (See Appendix A for a complete history of the Passover celebration.)

An Essene Baptism Ceremony

Summary

This then was the Jerusalem of Jesus' day—an occupied city attempting to maintain its Jewish character under the combined oppression of Roman rule and Hellenizing influences. Even their kings were Idumeans rather than descendants of Jacob. The city was swept with numerous undercurrents which made unification virtually impossible. These were indeed the last days as far as the nation of Israel was concerned. In A.D. 70 the Roman armies would eradicate the last vestiges of Old Testament worship as it had been practiced for fifteen hundred years. It was entirely fitting that this should be the place where Jesus would die in fulfillment of the law and where, like a phoenix, the plan of salvation would burst forth. It was here that Jesus would spend the last Passover of his life. It was from here, forty days later, that he would ascend from this earth with the promise to return for those who throughout the ensuing centuries would believe on his name. Heaven for mankind would be made possible by the events which would occur during a brief period of less than one hundred hours.

* * * * *

O Jerusalem, Jerusalem, you who kill the prophets and stone those sent to you, how often I have longed to gather your children together, as a hen gathers her chicks under her wings, but you were not willing. Look, your house is left to you desolate. For I tell you, you will not see me again until you say, "Blessed is he who comes in the name of the Lord."

Matthew 23:37–39

CHAPTER TWO

Jesus and His Disciples

The Passover Plot

John 11:55 When it was almost time for the Jewish Passover, many went up from the country to Jerusalem for their ceremonial cleansing before the Passover.
56 They kept looking for Jesus, and as they stood in the temple area they asked one another, "What do you think? Isn't he coming to the Feast at all?"
57 But the chief priests and Pharisees had given orders that if anyone found out where Jesus was, he should report it so that they might arrest him.
12:1 Six days before the Passover, Jesus arrived at Bethany, where Lazarus lived, whom Jesus had raised from the dead.

Jesus arrived at Bethany, two miles outside Jerusalem, as a man with a price on his head. With him were twelve disciples who had spent three years at his side and a group of women from Galilee among whom were Mary, his mother; Mary Magdalene, a woman out of whom he had cast seven demons; Salome, the mother of James and John; Mary, the mother of James the Less; and Joanna, wife of Herod's steward. Due to the overcrowding of the city during the Passover, they chose to stay in the village of Bethany where friends took in the various members of his party. On what has become known as Palm Sunday, Jesus entered Jerusalem and spent the better part of the week teaching in the temple. His enemies wanted to take him, but there simply was not an opportunity to do so because of the number of supporters constantly surrounding him. Thus, they were forced to wait for something to happen that would give them the opportunity they

The Old City as seen from the Mount of Olives

Jesus and His Disciples

sought. That something was not long in coming. Toward the middle of the week, a dinner was planned for Jesus and his disciples in one of the homes in Bethany. There began the series of events which led directly to his death on the cross.

At Dinner in Bethany

John 12:2 Here a dinner was given in Jesus' honor. Martha served, while Lazarus was among those reclining at the table with him. (Matt. 26:6)
    3 Then Mary took about a pint of pure nard, an expensive perfume; she poured it on Jesus' feet and wiped his feet with her hair. And the house was filled with the fragrance of the perfume. (Mark 14:3; Matt. 26:7)
    4 But one of his disciples, Judas Iscariot, who was later to betray him, objected,
    5 "Why wasn't this perfume sold and the money given to the poor? It was worth a year's wages." (Mark 14:4–5; Matt. 26:8–9)
    6 He did not say this because he cared about the poor but because he was a thief; as keeper of the money bag, he used to help himself to what was put into it.
    7 "Leave her alone," Jesus replied. "It was meant that she should save this perfume for the day of my burial. (Matt. 26:10; Mark 14:6)
    8 You will always have the poor among you, but you will not always have me. (Matt. 26:11; Mark 14:7)
Mark 14:8 She did what she could. She poured perfume on my body beforehand to prepare for my burial.
    9 I tell you the truth, wherever the gospel is preached throughout the world, what she has done will also be told, in memory of her." (Matt. 26:13)

This rebuke was evidently enough to cause Judas to decide to turn Jesus over to his enemies. All he needed was the opportunity to make his arrangements and then wait for a time to deliver him

Roman Coins

over when it would not attract the attention of the multitudes. Meanwhile, Jesus continued to spend his days teaching in the temple and his nights in Bethany. It was in Jerusalem that Judas found the opportunity to set his plan into motion.

Thirty Pieces of Silver

Luke 22:1	Now the Feast of Unleavened Bread, called the Passover, was approaching, (Matt. 26:1–2)
Matt. 26:3	Then the chief priest and the elders of the people assembled in the palace of the high priest, whose name was Caiaphas,
4	and they plotted to arrest Jesus in some sly way and kill him. (Mark 14:1; Luke 22:2)
5	"But not during the Feast," they said, "or there may be a riot among the people." (Mark 14:2)
Luke 22:3	Then Satan entered Judas, called Iscariot, one of the Twelve.
4	And Judas went to the chief priests and the officers of the temple guard and discussed with them how he might betray Jesus. (Matt. 26:14; Mark 14:10)
Matt. 26:15	"What are you willing to give me if I hand him over to you?"
Luke 22:5	They were delighted and agreed to give him money. (Mark 14:11)
Matt. 26:15	So they counted out for him thirty silver coins.
Luke 22:6	He consented, and watched for an opportunity to hand Jesus over to them when no crowd was present. (Matt. 26:16)

Jesus and His Disciples

The Road From Bethany

Prelude to Glory
The Twelve

Jesus and his disciples spent the last night in Bethany and the following morning rose to go into the city to celebrate the Passover. At his side walked the women who had come up with him from Galilee, the eleven he had chosen to be his special ambassadors, and the traitor, Judas Iscariot.

The Inner Circle. Peter, James, and John formed what is sometimes referred to as the inner circle. These three were possibly the closest to Jesus on this earth. Only these three were with him at the raising of Jairus' daughter and at the transfiguration, and these were the three he took with him into the Garden of Gethsemane. They were among the more affluent of the twelve. They had servants (Mark 1:16–20) and some believe, based on John 19:27, that in addition to his home in Capernaum, John also owned a home in Jerusalem. These three were partners in a fishing business along with Peter's brother, Andrew. They owned a fleet of fishing vessels on the Sea of Galilee, but Jesus had promised to make them fishers of men.

Peter

Born in Bethsaida, Peter was the son of Jonas (Matt. 16:17) and Johanna (tradition). His given name was Simon, meaning "hearer," but Jesus changed it to Peter (Greek) or Cephas (Hebrew), meaning "a stone." He was married and was generally spokesman for the twelve. His speech was distinctly Galilean. He was noted for his prompt energy, boldness, endurance, and enthusiasm—a "natural born leader." He was also impulsive and impetuous, short-tempered, prone to the use of foul language, lying upon occasion, and generally acting without thinking. During the next seventy-two hours he would:

1. refuse to have his feet washed by Jesus, then go to the opposite extreme and demand to be washed all over;
2. offer to die with Jesus, then deny he knew him;
3. attack the Roman soldiers who came to arrest Jesus (actually cutting off a man's ear) in an ill-advised attempt to prevent

Jesus' arrest, then flee in terror along with the rest of the apostles; and
4. swear in anger at being accused of knowing Jesus, then weep in bitter remorse for having done so.

Following the resurrection of Jesus he would be the first of the apostles to:

1. enter the empty tomb.
2. see the resurrected Christ.
3. preach the Gospel.
4. perform a miracle.
5. speak before the Sanhedrin.
6. preach to the Gentiles.
7. raise the dead.

He would write two epistles while, according to tradition, preaching the Gospel in Corinth, Babylon, Edessa, Nisibis, Colosse, Antioch, Pontus, and Rome. Tradition attributes his death to crucifixion in Rome between A.D. 60 and A.D. 65.

John

John, the youngest of the twelve, and his brother were named Sons of Thunder by Jesus. They were born to Zebedee (Matt. 4:21) and Salome (Matt. 27:56). John was originally a disciple of John the Baptist but followed Jesus when he learned of his superiority to the Baptist. He was a personal friend of the high priest, Caiaphas, and was known to the maid who kept the gate to the palace. He referred to himself as the "disciple whom Jesus loved." Following the resurrection, he made Jerusalem his chief residence but spent his last years in Ephesus. After fleeing from the Garden of Gethsemane, he and Peter would be the first to return and John, at least, would stay near Jesus during his trials and crucifixion.

John was the apostle into whose hands Jesus placed the care of his mother, Mary. John had brought her to the cross and was standing at her side when Jesus died. The rest of her life was spent as a member of his household. He was the first of the apostles to arrive at the empty tomb, though he did not enter until after Peter.

Prelude to Glory

In the last years of his life, he was banished to the Isle of Patmos for "the word of God" by either Nero (A.D. 65) or Domitian (A.D. 95). Tradition says that he was the only apostle to die of old age, probably in Ephesus around the turn of the century. He would write one of the four Gospels, three epistles, and the book of Revelation.

James

James was the older brother of John. He would have the dubious distinction of being the first apostle to die for his Lord. He was beheaded with a sword, then his corpse was thrown from a pinnacle of the temple by the order of Herod Agrippa I in A.D. 44. Roman legend says that he had preached in Spain and that his remains were sent there for burial.

Matthew and Simon the Zealot

Matthew and Simon the Zealot were diametrical opposites. There is no greater example of Christians putting aside their personal differences to work together than that of these two. One of the unrecognized miracles of the Bible is the fact that Simon did not kill Matthew at his first opportunity, because Matthew represented everything that Simon hated. He was what Simon considered the most loathsome of characters, one who, for the sake of personal gain, would assist the Romans in extracting the oppressive taxes from his fellow countrymen. Matthew was probably despised by all Jews but especially so by one as nationalistic as Simon. As a Zealot, Simon had been deeply involved in the rebellious cause of opposing Roman rule and stood for "the honor of the Law and the Israelite Theocracy." Only the love of Christ could bring these two together.

Matthew

Matthew was the son of Alphaeus and was also called Levi. His name meant "the gift of Jehovah." He lived in Capernaum and worked at the "Receipt of Customs" on the highly traveled road between Damascus and the Phoenician seaports. He was an opportunist who would cast his lot with whoever was of the most benefit at the moment. It is interesting to note that once he selected Jesus, he never wavered from his decision. Eustathius writes that after the Lord's ascension, Matthew preached in Judea, then in Ethiopia. Toward the end of his life, he wrote the "Gospel for the Jews," in which he argued from the Old Testament that Jesus is the Messiah, the Son of God. Tradition says he was slain with a sword in Ethiopia.

Simon the Zealot

Little is known of Simon beyond what the term "Zealot" tells us. He was possibly a cousin of Jesus, although this cannot be substantiated. Eusebius makes him Simon, the son of Clopas, who succeeded James as bishop in the Jerusalem church when it was moved to Pella following the Jewish persecution in which Stephen died. Eusebius further states that he was "martyred (by crucifixion) in his 120th year, under Trajan (A.D. 107), as a descendant of David who might claim the throne and give trouble to the Romans."

Andrew, Philip, and Bartholomew

Very little is known about Andrew, Philip, and Bartholomew except what is revealed in the New Testament and what has been handed down through tradition.

Andrew was the brother of Peter and a disciple of John the Baptist. Perhaps the greatest service he performed during the lifetime of Jesus was to bring his brother Peter into the group. Tradition says he carried the Gospel to Asia Minor, Greece, and Russia before being crucified at Patro in Archaia.

Philip was born in Capernaum but was living in Bethsaida during the ministry of Jesus. It was Philip who brought Bartholomew to Jesus. He became a disciple four days after John the Baptist identified Jesus as "Lord of Lords." Tradition says he carried the Gospel to central Asia Minor, where he was hanged against a pillar at Hieropolis.

Bartholomew was also called Nathaniel. He was a resident of Cana and a son of Tolmia. He displayed prejudice when told the

Messiah was Jesus of Nazareth by saying, "Can any good thing come out of Nazareth?" It was with regard to Bartholomew that Jesus said, "Behold, an Israelite indeed in whom there is no guile." Tradition says he preached in Parthis (an ancient kingdom southeast of the Caspian Sea) and in India before being flayed alive in Armenia.

Thomas, James the Less, and Thaddaeus

Thomas's Greek name was Didymus, which means "a twin." He was noted primarily as being cautious, thoughtful, skeptical, and gloomy. However, reading John 11:16 in which he is credited for saying, "Let us also go, that we may die with him," would cause one to add brave to the list. Thomas would be the last of the apostles to see the risen Lord. He demanded physical proof of the resurrection but upon seeing Jesus exclaimed, "My Lord and my God!" Tradition says he preached in Syria, Parthia, Persia, and India before being killed with a lance in the East Indies.

James the Less' father was also named Alphaeus, but there is no evidence that he and Matthew were brothers. He was a cousin of Jesus and the brother of Jude (possibly the writer of the book of Jude). James is also the probable writer of the book of James, although the evidence is not conclusive. Tradition says he preached in Palestine and Egypt before being clubbed to death in Jersualem shortly before its destruction in A.D. 70. His body was then decapitated before being buried.

Thaddaeus was also called Lebbaeus and Judas (not Iscariot). This is probably the same person as Jude, the brother of James and author of the book. Tradition says he preached in Syria, Arabia, and Mesopotamia before being shot to death with arrows in Edessa.

Judas Iscariot

Judas Iscariot was from Kerioth, a town in Judah. His father's name was Simon. He was the only apostle not from Galilee. It was he who would betray Jesus into the hands of his enemies. He was a thief according to John and was the keeper of the purse. He was avaricious, deceitful, and dishonest. Within twenty-four hours of his treachery, he would hang himself in a deserted place where his body would remain unnoticed until it became bloated to the point that when it dropped to the ground it "burst apart." His name will live in infamy as a synonym for treachery and his "kiss" as one of death.

The Women

When Jesus arrived in Jerusalem he had in his company of supporters a number of women who had come up with him from Galilee. Women were a part of his ministry from the beginning but most of the attention of the Gospel writers focused on the men. In the story of the resurrection, however, it is the women who come to the forefront and take center stage for the activities of that Sunday morning. Thus, it is important to understand who these women were and what their relationship was to Jesus and to his purpose.

Mary, the Mother of Jesus

Thirty-three years had passed since, as a young girl, Mary gave birth to her first child in the stable at Bethlehem. She had watched him grow to manhood, knowing within her heart that her child was more than just a man. Somewhere along the way she had lost her husband, Joseph. Tradition says that her sister, also called Mary, had been widowed also and the two raised their children together. Mary was now fifty or more years of age which was considered fairly old in that day and time. She had come on this last journey with Jesus just as she had on many previous ones.

No mother could read Mary's story without being cut to the heart by her pain. Within a few hours she saw her son arrested, tried and condemned, then publicly humiliated and crucified. She stood before the cross as he committed her to the care of John and his soul to God. She was there when they laid him in the grave and rolled the stone into place. She knew the agony and grief of those ensuing hours that every mother has felt who has ever seen her child laid to rest. Next to Jesus himself, Mary may well have paid a greater price for the salvation of mankind than any other person who has ever lived. Her reward came, however, when early on Sunday morning the word came that he had been resurrected and was alive. There can be no doubt that Jesus would spend part of the forty days following his resurrection comforting Mary. John tells us that she spent the remainder of her life as a member of his household. There is no further mention made of her following the Gospel accounts other than a brief mention in Acts 1.

Mary, the Mother of James

Mary, the Mother of James was also called Mary of Cleophas or Alphaeus, two names by which her husband was called. Many manuscripts distinguish between the two by referring to Jesus' mother as Mariam while referring to James's mother as Maria. That the two were sisters can be seen by a comparison of Matthew 27:56; Mark 15:40; and John 19:25.

Mary was the mother of seven children. Two of her sons, James the Less and Jude, were selected by Jesus as apostles. She also was present with her sister during the hours of ordeal and darkness. She helped prepare the spices with which to anoint Jesus' body and was one of the three women who arose before dawn to go to the tomb on Sunday morning. She and Salome were the two women who first saw the angels at the tomb and first heard the resurrection message.

Salome

Salome was the wife of Zebedee and the mother of the apostles James and John. She had also been with Jesus during most of his travels. It was she who requested that in his kingdom her sons be allowed to sit, one on his right hand and the other on his left. Present throughout the affair, she along with James' mother would be the first to hear the resurrection story from the angels. They would then carry the message to the apostles who were in hiding in the city.

Joanna

Joanna was the wife of Herod's steward, Chuza. We are told that she ministered of her substance to Jesus (Luke 8:3). She was with Jesus during the second tour of Galilee along with Mary Magdalene and many others. She is mentioned as being with the group of women to whom Jesus appeared following his resurrection but is not mentioned at the cross or tomb.

Mary Magdalene

Mary Magdalene occupies a prominent position among the women mentioned by the Gospel writers. She had become a devoted follower of Jesus when he cast seven demons out of her. She was present at the cross and at the burial. She helped with the preparation of spices to anoint the body and late on the Sabbath visited the tomb along with Mary the mother of James. She was one of the three who went to the tomb while it was still dark on Sunday morning. She was not present when the angels were first seen because, upon finding the tomb open and empty, she had run to bring Peter and John. Her faithfulness was rewarded, however, when, after Peter and John had come and gone, she became the first person to see the resurrected Christ.

These, then, were five of the women who participated in the events surrounding the death, burial, and resurrection of Jesus. From the beginning of the church women have played a prominent role in its growth. Women have always seemed more ready to accept the Gospel than men have. I have known congregations in which there were no men, but I have never known a congregation in which there were no women. Thus it should come as no surprise that while the apostles were hiding behind locked doors, the women were busy ministering to the Lord and bringing word of his resurrection to the world.

Jesus' Passover

There has been considerable discussion among scholars as to whether the "last supper" was a Passover celebration or just a meal which Jesus shared with his disciples. It is impossible to consider this question without first having a thorough understanding of the history of the Jewish Passover celebration. Appendix A is a study of that history. Anyone not thoroughly familiar with this subject should read Appendix "A" before continuing with this chapter.

In considering the last supper, this study will address the question in two parts.

1. Was the last supper a Passover celebration?
2. If so, was it celebrated on the same day as the Jewish national observance?

Logic simply will not support the position that the last supper was merely a regular meal Jesus ate with his disciples prior to his death. A careful consideration of all the facts shows conclusively that the last supper *was* a Passover celebration.

Support from the Gospel Record

The disciples asked Jesus, "Where do you want us to go and make preparations for you to eat the Passover?" (Matt. 26:17; Mark 14:12). Jesus told Peter and John to "go and make preparations for us to eat the Passover" (Luke 22:8). Peter and John went and "prepared the Passover" (Matt. 26:19; Mark 14:16). The Gospel writers state specifically that the meal was a Passover celebration.

Support from Jewish Tradition

The meal itself appears to have been very similar to the traditional Jewish Passover meal as it was celebrated in Jesus' day. The seating at the Passover meal was prescribed by rabbinic tradition wherein the guests were seated by rank or importance, and this may have been the source of contention among the apostles as to who would be the greatest in the Kingdom (Luke 22:24). Likewise, it seems the traditional prayers were said over the bread and wine. The traditional Jewish Passover required four separate cups of wine for each person, but this was by rabbinic decree, not divine command, and apparently Jesus used a single cup which was passed among the guests. Both the bread and the sop were parts of the traditional Passover meal, as was the custom of ending the meal with the singing of a hymn. Thus, with the possible exception of the manner in which the wine was served, all aspects of the meal described answer to the traditional Jewish Passover meal as it was celebrated in Jesus' day.

Support from Ancient Commandments

While the meal did in fact bear similarity to a traditional Passover meal of Jesus' day, it retained those elements which had originally been commanded by God. A careful study of the meal reveals that Jesus hosted the celebration of a Passover meal which adhered to God's prescriptions while, at the same time, allowing room for traditions God had not made a matter of command.

Jesus limited participation in the meal to the twelve. This would have been in keeping with the ancient manner of celebrating the Passover in the family context. Numerous others had come up with Jesus from Galilee but he held attendance at this meal to his immediate "spiritual" family. Others, such as Mark, whose home they may have been using, Nicodemus, and Joseph of Arimathea were all in Jerusalem but were not included in the meal. To do so would have violated the "family" context of the celebration.

Because of some differences between this meal, as described by the Gospel writers, and the traditional Passover meal of Jesus' day, some have doubted that this was a Passover meal at all. On the contrary, it was the only manner of celebration of the Passover which would have been acceptable to God.

Another thing that has caused many people to doubt that Jesus ate the Passover is the statement in John 18:28 which indicates Jesus ate the last supper the day *before* the Jews ate the Passover. They claim that this proves Jesus did not celebrate the Passover because he could not have had the lamb sacrificed before three o'clock the following afternoon, which was the official day and time for the sacrifice of the Passover lambs in the temple. This argument fails when consideration is given to the fact that in ancient times the lamb was sacrificed within the family context, not at the temple. Peter and John could have easily taken care of this as a part of their preparation of the Passover.

The only possible conclusion in view of the evidence is that Jesus indeed celebrated the Passover with his disciples on the night prior to his arrest and at the conclusion of that meal instituted the Lord's Supper which will be discussed in a subsequent chapter.

Prelude to Glory
The Day Jesus Celebrated the Passover

The argument has been made that if Jesus did celebrate the Passover, he had to do so at the same time as the rest of the Jewish nation. This argument fails when consideration is given to the fact that, while the scriptures are not entirely clear about how much of the Passover celebration was commandment and how much was tradition, there was certainly *no such confusion in the mind of Jesus of Nazareth*. The fact is, the Old Testament commands the Passover lamb be killed and eaten immediately after the sunset which begins the *fourteenth* of Nisan, the day upon which Jesus observed the Passover. There is no reason to believe Jesus would have changed this simply to comply with current Jewish tradition. We can be sure that Jesus ate the Passover at the precise day and time commanded by God, irrespective of what any rabbis or other scholars may have taught or written on the subject. This argument alone is conclusive. Even so, there is ample additional evidence available to support the fact that Jesus celebrated the Passover on the day before it was celebrated by the Jewish nation.

Support from the Gospel Record

According to John, the Jews had not yet eaten the Passover when they delivered Jesus to Pilate (John 18:28). John also states that it was "before the Passover Feast" that Jesus ate the meal in question (John 13:1). Mark says it was on the "evening" of the "first day of the Feast of Unleavened Bread, when it was customary to sacrifice the Passover lamb" that Jesus ate the meal in question (Mark 14:12, 17). It must be remembered that evening *began* the Jewish day. Luke says it was "the day of Unleavened Bread on which the Passover lamb had to be sacrificed" (Luke 22:7). The Jews ate the meal on the day *after* the sacrifice was made (that is, after sundown); therefore, Jesus ate his Passover the day before the Jewish nation did.

Jesus' trials and crucifixion took place on the day of "Preparation" according to Matthew 27:62; John 19:31; Mark 15:42; and Luke 23:54. While it has been argued that this term refers to Friday because that is when preparation was made for the seventh-day Sabbath, the same term was also used to refer to the day of preparation of the Passover, the day the animals were slaughtered, because the day after that was *also* a Sabbath, regardless of the day of the week on which it fell.

Support from Jewish Tradition

The Jews of the first century celebrated the *fifteenth* of Nisan as a Sabbath. The lamb was always slain on the afternoon of the *fourteenth;* therefore, the day in which the lamb was eaten, the *fifteenth,* was a Sabbath. The day on which the lamb was killed and eaten in Old Testament times (the fourteenth of Nisan) was declared by God to be a Sabbath (Lev. 23:7). So when the Jews changed the time of the sacrifice and the day on which it was eaten, they also changed the Sabbath. This being the case, had Jesus eaten the Passover in the same night as the Jewish nation, that day would have been a Sabbath. It is highly improbable that the kinds of activities that took place later that night and during the next morning would have been carried out on a Sabbath.

Since the Jewish day ended and began at sunset, the day on which Jesus ate the Passover and the day he was crucified were one and the same. The most convincing argument against that day's being a Sabbath comes from the Jews themselves. The Jewish authorities went to Pilate, while Jesus was still on the cross, and requested that the legs of the prisoners be broken in order to speed up their deaths. This was not due to any compassion on the part of the Jews. Their stated reason was that they did not want the bodies hanging on the cross during the Sabbath. If they wanted them off the cross *before* the Sabbath began, then it is obvious the day then coming to an end was *not* a Sabbath. And, if it was *not* a Sabbath, it was *not* the day on which the Jews ate the Passover meal.

Conclusion

Logic, the Gospel writers, and Jewish tradition all argue against Jesus' having celebrated the Passover on the same day as the Jewish nation. Jesus celebrated the Passover on the fourteenth of Nisan in accordance with the ancient commands of God which were never rescinded. The Jewish nation celebrated the Passover on the fifteenth of Nisan in accordance with the teaching of their rabbis. There is therefore no contradiction between John and the synoptic writers on this point.

Summary

This then was the band of disciples which stood with Jesus on the Mount of Olives as he prepared to enter Jerusalem to celebrate the Passover. Jesus would celebrate this Passover with them and then be arrested, tried, and crucified. This he knew, but it would be at a time and place of his choosing, not that of his enemies. His hour was near, but not yet come. To ensure that he would have this Passover with his disciples without interruption, he had taken care of one last detail before leaving the city the day before. A signal had been arranged by which his disciples (Peter and John, but not Judas) would know where the Passover meal would be celebrated. Jesus would bring the others there when the time for the supper arrived. For now, they stood outside the gate to the city. Within awaited the salvation of mankind. Events from this point forward would be under Jesus' direct control and would unfold exactly in accordance with the divine plan formulated prior to the laying of the foundations of the earth.

Anyone who loves his father or mother more than me is not worthy of me; . . . anyone who loves his son or daughter more than me is not worthy of me; and anyone who does not take his cross and follow me is not worthy of me. Whoever finds his life will lose it, and whoever loses his life for my sake will find it.

Matthew 10:37–39

CHAPTER THREE

At Supper with the Twelve

Mark 14:12 On the first day of the Feast of Unleavened Bread, when it was customary to sacrifice the Passover lamb, Jesus' disciples asked him, "Where do you want us to go and make preparations for you to eat the Passover?" (Luke 22:7; Matt. 26:17)

Luke 22:8 Jesus sent Peter and John, saying, "Go and make preparations for us to eat the Passover." (Mark 14:13)

9 "Where do you want us to prepare for it?" they asked.

10 He replied, "As you enter the city, a man carrying a jar of water will meet you. Follow him to the house that he enters,

11 and say to the owner of the house, 'The Teacher asks: Where is the guest room, where I may eat the Passover with my disciples?' (Mark 14:14; Matt. 26:18)

12 He will show you a large upper room, all furnished. Make preparations there." (Mark 14:15)

13 They left and found things just as Jesus had told them. So they prepared the Passover. (Mark 14:16; Matt. 26:19).

Making Ready the Passover

The Bread. The fourteenth through the twenty-first of Nisan was called the Feast of Unleavened Bread. Only bread without yeast could be eaten during this eight-day period. On the evening before, the head of each house made an elaborate search for any

Prelude to Glory

The Last Supper

leaven (yeast) or leavened bread. The house had to be entirely empty of yeast and bread made with yeast prior to midnight.

The Meat. Business would be brisk in the cattle market near the temple where the lambs for the Passover meal were sold. These lambs had to be at least eight days old and not more than one year old. They also had to be perfect in every way.

The sacrificial ceremony for the slaying of the Passover lamb began at three o'clock. All of the twenty-four courses of priests were on duty at the temple so all the lambs could be killed and sacrificed during the afternoon. Not less than ten people were to share one lamb, but often many more were included in the group.

Three identical sacrifices were conducted. At the beginning of each sacrifice, every Jew with a lamb killed it at a given signal. The blood was caught in a golden bowl, passed on by a chain of living hands, and poured out at the altar. The animals were then skinned and cleaned, and the inside fat was taken out and burned on the altar. During all this time, the Levites led in song, and when they were done, the people were dismissed to make way for the next group.

The lamb had to be roasted on a spit made of pomegranate wood. Great care had to be taken so that the lamb did not touch the stove and that no bones were broken. The lamb had to be roasted on the fire with head, tail, and legs intact, and then served on a large platter. The entire lamb had to be consumed, and any portion not eaten had to be burned.

The Wine. The use of wine for the Passover supper, though not mentioned in the law, was strictly enjoined by tradition. According to the Jerusalem Talmud, it was intended to express Israel's joy on the Paschal Night, and even the poorest was required to have "at least four cups, though he were to receive the money for it from the poor's box" (Mishnah, Pes. 10.1). "If he cannot otherwise obtain it," the Talmud adds, "He must sell or pawn his coat, or hire himself out for these four cups of wine." Red wine alone was to be used at the Passover supper and was always mixed half and half with water. Each of the four cups a person drank contained one half pint.

The Bitter Herbs. The Mishnah mentions only five kinds as falling within the designation of "bitter herbs"—lettuce, endive, succory, beets, and bitter corriander. The "bitter herbs" were partaken of twice during the meal—once dipped in salt water, and a second time with "charoseth," a compound of dates, raisins, ground nuts, and vinegar, though the Mishnah expressly declares that the charoseth was not obligatory.

Prelude to the Supper

Mark 14:17 When evening came, Jesus arrived with the Twelve.

Late in the afternoon, Jesus and his disciples came to the upper room. Had this been on the day of the national observance, a threefold blast of the shofar's horn, blown at the temple just after sunset, would have told the people the time for the meal had come. The house in which Jesus celebrated the "Last Supper" is commonly believed to have been the home of John Mark, the same Mark who would become the author of the second Gospel and a missionary companion with Paul and Barnabas.

Luke 22:14 When the hour came, Jesus and his apostles reclined at the table. (Matt. 26:20).
15 And he said to them, "I have eagerly desired to eat this Passover with you before I suffer.
16 For I tell you, I will not eat it again until it finds fulfillment in the kingdom of God."
Luke 22:24 Also a dispute arose among them as to which of them was considered to be greatest.

As mentioned earlier, many commentators believe this contention arose regarding who would occupy which positions at the Passover table, and the context of Luke 22:25–30 appears to confirm this belief.

Guests at the Paschal Table

As the guests gathered around the Passover table, they came no longer, as at the first celebration, with their loins girded, with shoes on their feet and a staff in their hand—that is, as travellers

At Supper with the Twelve

**The Shofar's Blast
Heralds the Sabbath**

**The Coenaculum—
Room of the Last Supper**

waiting to take their departure. On the contrary, they were arrayed in their best festive garments and were joyous and at rest, as became the children of a king. To express this idea the rabbis also insisted that the Paschal Supper—or at least part of it—be eaten in that recumbent position with which we are familiar from the New Testament. They used this leaning posture, as free men do, in memorial of their freedom, and because it was the manner of slaves to eat standing. Therefore they ate sitting and leaning, in order to show they had been delivered from bondage into freedom. But though it was deemed desirable to sit leaning during the whole Paschal Supper, it was only absolutely required while partaking of the bread and wine. This recumbent posture resembled that still common in the East, where the body rests on the feet. Hence, the penitent woman at the feast given by Simon is said to have "stood behind him at his feet weeping" (Luke 7:38). At the same time, the left elbow was placed on the table, and the head rested on the hand, sufficient room being left between each guest for the free movement of the right hand. This explains in what sense John was "leaning on Jesus' bosom" and afterwards "lying on Jesus' breast" when he bent back to speak to Him (John 13:23, 25 KJV).

Seating at the Paschal Table

The traditional Jewish Passover table was about fifteen to eighteen inches high, and surrounded with pillows upon which the guests reclined.

The host at the dinner would occupy the second position from the left. The youngest person present would occupy the position immediately to the left of the host and the "chief guest" would be seated to the host's immediate right (as seen from across the table). Beginning with the chief guest, the others would occupy the remaining positions going to the right in order of importance. Thus, the person of least importance would be in the utmost seat to the right or, in the case of an oval or U-shaped table, a position directly across from the youngest, the end at which the youngest and least sat being left vacant.

Jesus, as host, would have taken the assigned position and John, who must indeed have been the youngest as tradition

At Supper with the Twelve

SEATING AT THE PASCHAL TABLE

| John | Jesus | Judas | ? | ? | ? |

| Paschal Table | Dining Table | ? |

| Peter | ? | ? | ? | ? | ? |

Diagram—Seating at the Last Supper

holds, would have been seated in the first position, next to Jesus.

The contention, then, concerned who would occupy the remaining positions around the table, and in what order. Jesus seized upon this opportunity to teach a lesson in service in the kingdom.

Luke 22:25 Jesus said to them, "The kings of the Gentiles lord it over them; and those who exercise authority over them call themselves Benefactors.
26 But you are not to be like that. Instead, the greatest among you should be like the youngest, and the one who rules like the one who serves.
27 For who is greater, the one who is at the table or the one who serves? Is it not the one who is at the table? But I am among you as one who serves.
28 You are those who have stood by me in my trials.
29 And I confer on you a kingdom, just as my Father conferred one on me,
30 So that you may eat and drink at my table in my kingdom and sit on thrones, judging the twelve tribes of Israel."

This lesson in service, as we shall see later in this study, resulted in Peter's taking one of the lowest seats while only Judas was presumptuous enough to take the chief seat.

Prelude to Glory
Celebrating the Passover

The prayer to be recited over the first cup was strictly prescribed by Jewish tradition.

> Blessed art thou, O Lord our God, who hast created the fruit of the vine! Blessed art thou, O Lord our God, King of the universe, who has chosen us from among all people, and exalted us from among all languages, and sanctified us with thy commandments! And thou has given us, O Lord our God, in love, the solemn days for joy, and the festivals and appointed seasons for gladness; this, the day of the Feast of Unleavened Bread, the season of our freedom, a holy convocation, the memorial of our departure from Egypt. For us has thou chosen; and us has thou sanctified from among all nations, and thy holy festivals with joy and with gladness has thou caused us to inherit. Blessed art thou, O Lord who sanctifies Israel and the appointed seasons! Blessed art thou, O Lord, King of the universe, who has preserved us alive and sustained us and brought us to this season!

Luke 22:17 After taking the cup, he gave thanks and said, "Take this and divide it among you.
     18 For I tell you I will not drink again of the fruit of the vine until the kingdom of God comes."

The first cup of wine was drunk, and each washed his hands.

Washing the Disciples' Feet

The ritual of the "first cup" now being complete, it is commonly believed that Jesus took advantage of the pause to continue the lesson in service and humility which he had begun during the disagreement over the seating.

Washing the feet of guests in a Jewish home was a common custom in Jesus' day. It was considered to be a means of extending hospitality as well as according honor. The task, however, was always performed by the most menial of the household servants, never by the master of the house. Thus Mary Magdalene had on a previous occasion, as a demonstration of humility, washed Jesus' feet with her tears and dried them with her hair.

At Supper with the Twelve

John 13:1 It was just before the Passover Feast. Jesus knew that the time had come for him to leave this world and go to the Father. Having loved his own who were in the world, he now showed them the full extent of his love.
    2 The evening meal was being served, and the devil had already prompted Judas Iscariot, son of Simon, to betray Jesus.
    3 Jesus knew that the Father had put all things under his power, and that he had come from God and was returning to God;
    4 so he got up from the meal, took off his outer clothing, and wrapped a towel around his waist.

Such girding was the common mark of a slave by whom the service of footwashing was ordinarily performed.

John 13:5 After that, he poured water into a basin and began to wash his disciples' feet, drying them with the towel that was wrapped around him.
    6 He came to Simon Peter, who said to him, "Lord, are you going to wash my feet?"
    7 Jesus replied, "You do not realize now what I am doing, but later you will understand."
    8 "No," said Peter, "you shall never wash my feet."

Peter, having already taken a lower seat at the table to demonstrate his own humility, was unable to accept the idea that the man he considered to be "the Christ"—"The Son of the Living God"—would humble himself in such a manner, particularly not at the feet of one who considered himself so unworthy a servant as Peter did.

John 13:8 Jesus answered, "Unless I wash you, you have no part with me."

The idea of being so abruptly disowned by Jesus was even more unacceptable to Peter than Jesus' washing his feet. True to his well-known character, he then went to the opposite extreme.

John 13:9 "Then, Lord," Simon Peter replied, "not just my feet but my hands and my head as well!"
10 Jesus answered, "A person who has had a bath needs only to wash his feet; his whole body is clean. And you are clean, though not every one of you."
11 For he knew who was going to betray him, and that was why he said not every one was clean.

Jesus' obvious desire was to use this occasion to teach his disciples, yet from here on we see Judas Iscariot's presence increasingly distracting him and forcing him to limit the application of his teaching.

John 13:12 When he had finished washing their feet, he put on his clothes and returned to his place. "Do you understand what I have done for you?" he asked them.
13 "You call me 'Teacher' and 'Lord,' and rightly so, for that is what I am.
14 Now that I, your Lord and Teacher, have washed your feet, you also should wash one another's feet.
15 I have set you an example that you should do as I have done for you.
16 I tell you the truth, no servant is greater than his master, nor is a messenger greater than the one who sent him.
17 Now that you know these things, you will be blessed if you do them."

Again, Jesus, drawn away from concentrating on his teaching by the presence of Judas, felt compelled to limit the application of his words by saying:

John 13:18 "I am not referring to all of you; I know those I have chosen. But this is to fulfill the scripture: 'He who shares my bread has lifted up his heel against me.'
19 I am telling you now before it happens, so that when it does happen you will believe that I am He."

The scripture Jesus refers to here (Ps. 41:9) is one of more than 150 messianic prophecies contained in the Old Testament. The intent of Jesus' words was to keep before his apostles the proof of his claim to divinity. Temporarily forcing Judas from his mind, he returned to his subject.

John 13:20 "I tell you the truth, whoever accepts anyone I send accepts me; and whoever accepts me accepts the one who sent me."

The Paschal Table

The Paschal table was then brought forward. This was a separate table containing the herbs, two loaves of unleavened bread, and the Passover lamb. It was placed at the end of the larger table around which the guests were reclining, and in a position which would enable the host to reach all the articles easily. The host would then take up in succession the dish with the Passover lamb, that with the bitter herbs, and that with the unleavened bread and briefly explain the import of each. Rabbi Gamaliel, the teacher of Paul, wrote:

> Whoever does not explain three things in the Passover has not fulfilled the duty incumbent on him. These three things are: the Passover lamb, the unleavened bread, and the bitter herbs.
> The Passover lamb means that God passed over the blood-sprinkled place on the house of our fathers in Egypt.
> The unleavened bread means that our fathers were delivered out of Egypt in haste.
> The bitter herbs means that the Egyptians made bitter the lives of our fathers in Egypt. (Mish. Pes. 10.5)

The host would then take some of the herbs, dip them in salt water, and eat them. The herbs and the dish of salt water would then be passed around to each of the guests. The Paschal table would then be removed and the "second cup" would be filled.

The Second Cup

At this point in the service a ceremony took place which was required by the law (Ex. 13:8). At each Passover supper, the father, or host, was to show his son (or the youngest male present) the import of this festival. By way of carrying out this duty, the son, or youngest male, was directed at this particular part of the service to ask the question:

> "Why is this night distinguished from all other nights? For on all other nights we eat leavened or unleavened bread, but on this night only unleavened bread! On all other nights we eat any kind of herbs, but on this night only bitter herbs? On all other nights we eat meat roasted, stewed, or boiled, but on this night only roasted? On all other nights we dip (the herbs) only once, but on this night twice?"
>
> The father then instructs his son according to the capacity of his knowledge, "Beginning with our disgrace and ending with our glory." (Mish., Pes. X, 4)

The father began by quoting Deuteronomy 26:5–11 and, as he did so, explained to the best of his ability the whole national history, commencing with Terah, Abraham's father, and telling of his idolatry, and continuing, in due order, the story of Israel up to their deliverance from Egypt and the giving of the Law. The more fully he explained it, the better.

Regarding this dissertation, Rabbi Gamaliel wrote:

> From generation to generation every man is bound to look upon himself not otherwise than if he had himself come forth out of Egypt. For so is it, and thou shalt show thy son in that day, saying, this is done because of that which the Lord did unto me when I came forth out of Egypt.

The Mishnah further states:

> Therefore, we are bound to thank, praise, laud, glorify, extol, honor, bless, exalt, and reverence Him, because He hath wrought for our fathers, and for us all these miracles. He brought us forth from bondage into freedom, from sorrow into joy, from mourning to a festival, from darkness to a great light, and from slavery to redemption. Therefore let us sing before Him: Hallelujah! (Mish., Pes. 10.5)

Then the first part of the Hallel was sung, comprising Psalms 113 and 114, with this thanks at the close:

At Supper with the Twelve

He that redeemed us and redeemed our fathers from Egypt and brought us to this night to eat therein, unleavened bread and bitter herbs! Therefore O Lord our God and the God of our fathers, bring us in peace to the other set of feasts and festivals which are coming to meet us, while we rejoice in the building-up of the city and are joyful in thy worship; and may we eat there of the sacrifices and of the Passover-offering whose blood has reached with acceptance the wall of thy altar, and let us praise thee for our redemption and for the ransoming of our soul—Blessed art thou, O Lord who has redeemed Israel! (Mish., Pes. 10.6)

Following this, the second cup was drunk. Hands were washed a second time, with the same prayer as before. The Paschal table was then returned and one of the two unleavened cakes broken and thanks given.

Rabbinical authorities distinctly state that this thanksgiving was to follow, not to preceed, the breaking of the bread because it was the bread of poverty, "and the poor have not whole cakes, but broken pieces." This distinction is important, as proving that since the Lord first gave thanks and then broke the bread (Matt. 26:26; Mark 14:22; Luke 22:19; I Cor. 11:24), he instituted the Lord's Supper later in the service.

Judas Exposed

It was during this lengthened exposition and service that Jesus became "troubled in spirit," according to John's Gospel.

John 13:21 After he had said this, Jesus was troubled in spirit and testified, "I tell you the truth, one of you is going to betray me." (Mark 14:18)

Mark 14:18 ". . . one who is eating with me." (Matt. 26:21; Luke 22:21)

Matt. 26:22 They were very sad and began to say to him one after the other, "Surely not I, Lord?" (Mark 14:19)

23 Jesus replied, "The one who has dipped his hand into the bowl with me will betray me." (Mark 14:20)

Mark 14:21 "The Son of Man will go just as it is written about him. But woe to that man who betrays the Son of

	Man! It would be better for him if he had not been born." (Matt. 26:24; Luke 22:22)
Luke 22:23	They began to question among themselves which of them it might be who would do this. (John 13:22)
John 13:23	One of them, the disciple whom Jesus loved, was reclining next to him.
24	Simon Peter motioned to this disciple and said, "Ask him which one he means." (Luke 22:23)
25	Leaning back against Jesus, he asked him, "Lord, who is it?"
26	Jesus answered, "It is the one to whom I will give this piece of bread when I have dipped it in the dish."

This refers to pieces of the broken cake with bitter herbs between them, dipped in the charoseth. They were handed to each person following the prayer and second cup. Jesus, as host, would have been preparing to do this at this point in the service, and Judas, who was sitting next to him in the seat of the chief guest, would have been the one to whom Jesus passed it. This then, in all probability, was the "piece of bread" to which Jesus referred.

John 13:26	Then, dipping the piece of bread, he gave it to Judas Iscariot, son of Simon.
Matt. 26:25	Then Judas, the one who would betray him, said, "Surely not I, Rabbi?" Jesus answered, "Yes, it is you."
John 13:27	As soon as Judas took the bread, Satan entered into him. "What you are about to do, do quickly," Jesus told him,
28	but no one at the meal understood why Jesus said this to him.
29	Since Judas had charge of the money, some thought Jesus was telling him to buy what was needed for the Feast, or to give something to the poor.
30	As soon as Judas had taken the bread, he went out. And it was night.

The unleavened bread with bitter herbs constituted, in reality, the beginning of the Paschal Supper, to which the first part of the service had only served as a kind of introduction. But Judas "went out" after taking the bread. Therefore he could not even have participated in the eating of the Paschal lamb, much less the Lord's Supper which was to follow.

The Paschal Supper

The Paschal Supper itself consisted of the unleavened bread with bitter herbs, the so-called chagigah or peace offering (when brought), and lastly, of the Paschal lamb itself. After that, nothing more was to be eaten, so that the flesh of the Paschal sacrifice might be the last meat eaten. Then, having again washed hands, the third cup was filled and grace after meat was said. It is believed to have been at this point in the service that Jesus instituted "his Supper" by taking bread, blessing it, and then breaking it instead of adhering to the old injunction of not eating anything after the Passover lamb.

The Lord's Supper

Luke 22:19 And he took bread, gave thanks and broke it, and gave it to them, saying, "This is my body given for you; do this in remembrance of me." (Matt. 26:26; Mark 14:22)

20 In the same way, after the supper he took the cup saying, "This cup is the new covenant in my blood, which is poured out for you." (Matt. 26:27; Mark 14:23)

Matt. 26:28 "This is my blood of the covenant, which is poured out for many for the forgiveness of sins. (Mark 14:24)

29 "I tell you, I will not drink of this fruit of the vine from now on until that day when I drink it anew with you in my Father's kingdom." (Mark 14:25)

There cannot be any reasonable doubt that this third cup was the cup which Jesus connected with his own supper. It is called in

Jewish writings, as it was by the apostle Paul, "The Cup of Blessing" (I Cor. 10:16) partly because it and the first cup required a special blessing and partly because it followed the "Grace after Meat."

Concluding the Supper

The service concluded with the fourth cup, after which the second portion of the Hallel was sung, consisting of Psalms 115 through 118. The ceremony ended with the so-called "Blessing of the Song," which was comprised of two brief prayers.

> All Thy works shall praise thee, O Lord our God. And Thy saints, the righteous, who do Thy good pleasure, and all Thy people, the house of Israel, with joyous song let them praise, and bless, and magnify, and glorify, and exalt, and reverence, and sanctify, and ascribe the kingdom to Thy name, O our King! For it is good to praise Thee, and pleasure to sing praises unto Thy name, for from everlasting to everlasting Thou art God.

> The breath of all that lives shall praise Thy name, O Lord our God. And the spirit of all flesh shall continually glorify and exalt Thy memorial, O our King! For from everlasting to everlasting Thou art God, and besides Thee we have no King, Redeemer, or Savior.

This is the manner in which the Passover Supper was celebrated by the Jews at the time of Jesus.

The Last Discourse

Jesus Predicts Peter's Denial

Although he skips over the institution of the Lord's Supper, John does, by saying it was after Judas had departed, pinpoint for us when the discussion took place between Peter and Jesus concerning Peter's impending denials, the more complete details of the discussion being provided by the other writers.

Jesus had begun a lengthy discourse in John 13:31 but was interrupted almost immediately by Peter. Following the interrup-

At Supper with the Twelve

tion, John again picked up Jesus' discourse as it began in the upper room and related it to its completion some time later as the group arrived at the Mount of Olives. For the entire text of that discourse the reader should refer to the Gospel of John, chapters fourteen to seventeen. For purposes of this study we will include only the beginning of the discourse and the conversation which followed Peter's interruption.

John 13:31 When he was gone, Jesus said, "Now is the Son of Man glorified and God is glorified in him.
    32 If God is glorified in him, God will glorify the Son in himself, and will glorify him at once.
    33 My children, I will be with you only a little longer. You will look for me, and just as I told the Jews, so I tell you now: Where I am going, you cannot come.
    34 A new commandment I give you: Love one another. As I have loved you, so you must love one another.
    35 All men will know that you are my disciples if you love one another."
    36 Simon Peter asked him, "Lord, where are you going?" Jesus replied, "Where I am going, you cannot follow now, but you will follow later."
    37 Peter asked, "Lord, why can't I follow you now? I will lay down my life for you."
    38 Then Jesus answered, "Will you really lay down your life for me? I tell you the truth, before the rooster crows, you will disown me three times!"
Matt. 26:31 Then Jesus told them, "This very night you will all fall away on account of me, for it is written: I will strike the shepherd, and the sheep of the flock will be scattered." (Mark 14:27)
    32 But after I have risen, I will go ahead of you into Galilee." (Mark 14:28)
    33 Peter replied, "Even if all fall away on account of you, I never will." (Mark 14:29)
Mark 14:30 "I tell you the truth," Jesus answered, "today—yes, tonight—before the rooster crows twice you yourself will disown me three times."

Prelude to Glory

	31 But Peter insisted emphatically, "Even if I have to die with you, I will never disown you." And all the others said the same. (Matt. 26:35)
Luke 22:31	[Jesus said,] "Simon, Simon, Satan has asked to sift you as wheat.
	32 But I have prayed for you, Simon, that your faith will not fail. And when you have turned back, strengthen your brothers."
	33 But he replied, "Lord, I am ready to go with you to prison and to death."
	34 Jesus answered, "I tell you, Peter, before the rooster crows today, you will deny three times that you know me." (Matt. 26:34)
	35 Then Jesus asked them, "When I sent you without purse, bag or sandals, did you lack anything?" "Nothing," they answered.
	36 He said to them, "But now if you have a purse take it, and also a bag; and if you don't have a sword, sell your cloak and buy one.
	37 It is written: 'And he was numbered with the transgressors,' and I tell you that this must be fulfilled in me. Yes, what is written about me is reaching its fulfillment."
	38 The disciples said, "See, Lord, here are two swords." "That is enough," he replied.
Matt. 26:30	When they had sung a hymn, they went out to the Mount of Olives. (Mark 14:26; Luke 22:39)

* * * * *

For I received from the Lord what I also passed on to you: The Lord Jesus, on the night he was betrayed, took bread, and when he had given thanks, he broke it and said, "This is my body, which is for you; do this in remembrance of me." In the same way, after supper he took the cup, saying, "This cup is the new covenant in my blood; do this, whenever you drink it, in remembrance of me." For whenever you eat this bread and drink this cup, you proclaim the Lord's death until he comes.

I Corinthians 11:23–26

CHAPTER FOUR

Agony in the Garden

To the east of Jerusalem, across the Kidron Valley, lay the Mount of Olives. This had been a favorite place of Jesus' when in and around the city. It was on this mount earlier in the week that he sat with his disciples and told them about the upcoming destruction of Jerusalem and the signs they should look for to know when to flee from the city. It was from this mount some forty days later that Jesus would take his last steps on this earth and ascend to heaven. Now, as midnight drew near, he came here with the eleven to await the arrival of Satan's hour.

The Walk to Gethsemane

It took approximately thirty minutes to walk from the southwestern section of Jerusalem where the upper room was located to the Mount of Olives, depending on which of two possible routes Jesus took. The shortest of the two routes was to walk east through the upper city into the lower city and out through the gate which led to Bethany. From there it was merely a matter of crossing the Kidron Valley and walking partway up the side of the mount. The other route was to exit the city through the southern gate which led to the Hinnom Valley, then walk east around the outside of the wall until he came to the Bethany Gate.

While still in the upper room Jesus began a discussion in which he attempted to prepare his disciples for the drama that lay ahead. The cross was now only some nine hours away. From the time of the Garden of Eden it had been prophesied that Satan must have his moment of victory, and Jesus knew the difficulty this would pose for his disciples. He had already told them they would all disown him before the night was over. Peter in particular had been singled out as one who would deny him three times. As they

Garden of Gethsemane

Agony in the Garden

walked from the upper room to the Garden of Gethsemane Jesus continued that discussion, which is in chapters fourteen through seventeen of John, and finished it just as they crossed the Kidron Valley and entered the Garden of Gethsemane.

The Garden of Gethsemane

John 18:1 When he had finished praying, Jesus left with his disciples and crossed the Kidron Valley. On the other side there was an olive grove, and he and his disciples went into it. (Matt. 26:30; Mark 14:26; Luke 22:39)

Matt. 26:36 Then Jesus went with his disciples to a place called Gethsemane, and he said to them, "Sit here while I go over there and pray." (Mark 14:32)

As mentioned earlier the Garden of Gethsemane, probably surrounded by a stone fence at the time Jesus used it, was a private garden owned by a merchant who had an olive press set up in the midst of the olive groves that covered the mount. The owner may have either been a disciple or was at least sympathetic toward Jesus. It is also possible the owner was a friend of John's as John appears to have been well known among the wealthy and influential in Jerusalem (John 18:15).

Four sites compete today for the distinction of being the location of the Garden of Gethsemane. All, however, are in virtually the same area, so there is really little doubt of the approximate location of the original garden. From its vantage point about halfway up the Mount of Olives, there is a clear view across the Kidron Valley to the gate of the city. It would be impossible for anyone to leave the city and cross the Kidron Valley without being seen from the garden, especially if he carried lighted torches. Here Jesus chose to wait for the inevitable and went to the Father in prayer as he did so.

Luke 22:40 On reaching the place, he said to them, "Pray that you will not fall into temptation."

Matt. 26:37 He took Peter and the two sons of Zebedee along

Prelude to Glory

> with him, and he began to be sorrowful and troubled. (Mark 14:33)
>
> 38 Then he said to them, "My soul is overwhelmed with sorrow to the point of death. Stay here and keep watch with me." (Mark 14:34)

Eight of the disciples were left at the entrance to the garden with instructions to pray about temptation. Three disciples—Peter, James, and John—were taken farther into the garden and left with the instructions to watch and pray. They were evidently placed in a position which would allow them to see anyone approaching across the Kidron Valley. This is what Jesus meant for them to watch for. He also told them to pray, no doubt thinking about the temptation they were about to face. Jesus then went to a secluded spot where he could be alone and knelt in prayer.

The First Prayer

> **Mark 14:35** Going a little farther, he fell to the ground and prayed that if possible the hour might pass from him. (Matt. 26:39; Luke 22:41)
>
> 36 "*Abba*, Father," he said, "everything is possible for you. Take this cup from me. Yet not what I will, but what you will." (Matt. 26:39; Luke 22:42)
>
> **Luke 22:43** An angel from heaven appeared to him and strengthened him.
>
> 44 And being in anguish, he prayed more earnestly, and his sweat was like drops of blood falling to the ground.

Here, and in one statement on the cross, the humanity and weakness of his human form show through. Here we see not the God, but the man. The scriptures tell us that Jesus was in every way tempted just as we are and yet was without sin (Heb. 4:15). It was not his being God that sustained him through this agony, but rather, his confidence in God. Each person has the same ability to withstand temptation that Jesus had. Here in the Garden of Gethsemane only hours before his death, Jesus gave the perfect example of turning to God to supply that which is lacking in one's own abilities.

Agony in the Garden

The earnestness of that prayer can be seen in the fact that while we only know two short sentences, the entire prayer lasted an hour. It would have been nearing midnight when he rose from prayer to go back and check on Peter, James, and John.

> **Matt. 26:40** Then he returned to his disciples and found them sleeping. "Could you men not keep watch with me for one hour?" he asked Peter. (Mark 14:37; Luke 22:45)
> **41** "Watch and pray so that you will not fall into temptation. The spirit is willing, but the body is weak." (Mark 14:38; Luke 22:46)

The lateness of the hour, combined with four cups of wine at the Passover feast, could not help having an effect on the disciples. The temptation Jesus continued to warn them against was the temptation of disbelief which he knew was going to come upon them when they saw him taken by the soldiers and later as they saw him hang on the cross. Their concept of the messiah was of a conquering savior, not a suffering one. Later they would understand, but for the time being their faith and confidence in Jesus of Nazareth was about to be shattered. When they were awake, Jesus returned to his secluded place and continued to pray.

The Second Prayer

> **Matt. 26:42** He went away a second time and prayed, "My Father, if it is not possible for this cup to be taken away unless I drink it, may your will be done." (Mark 14:39)

The cup Jesus referred to was his death on the cross. It was the same cup he had referred to when James and John came to him to ask if one could sit on his right and the other on his left in his kingdom (Mark 10:38–39). It is obvious Jesus did not want to go to the cross. He did so for only two reasons. One was that it was the will of God, and that alone would have been reason enough. But Jesus had a second reason which should also be remembered. He had told his disciples that "Greater love has no one than this, that one lay down his life for his friends" (John 15:13). His second reason was his love of mankind. It has truly been said that love placed Jesus on the cross.

The Third Prayer

> **Matt. 26:43** When he came back, he again found them sleeping, because their eyes were heavy. (Mark 14:40)
> 44 So he left them and went away once more and prayed the third time, saying the same thing.
> 45 Then he returned to the disciples and said to them, "Are you still sleeping and resting? Look, the hour is near, and the Son of Man is betrayed into the hands of sinners." (Mark 14:41)

From his vantage point in the garden, Jesus was able to see the band of people approaching from the city long before they reached the place where he and the disciples were. It would have been no trouble to simply gather up the disciples and leave before Judas and the others with him arrived. That, however, was not the plan. Jesus had been in control from the beginning. He was still in control and he knew that the hour had now come. His entire life had been governed by the "hour" and he would not turn away from it now. Judas and the band would come and he would wait. They would do what they must in order to fulfill the scriptures, but he would be the one who was in control of the events, not them. Judas was leading the group. He had been very busy since leaving the upper room approximately three hours earlier.

The Trail of the Betrayer

There is a number of facts available that allow us to plot Judas' trail that night. An examination of the "timeline," which is Appendix B, shows Judas's movements and indicates he must have left the upper room at around nine o'clock in the evening in order to arrive at the garden shortly after midnight. The company that the Gospel writers tell us Judas had with him when he

Agony in the Garden

arrived at the garden gives us a very clear picture of where he must have been during this time. Named by the Gospel writers as being with him when he arrived at the garden were the following:

1. soldiers
2. a servant of the high priest
3. officials representing
   a. the captain of the temple
   b. the Pharisees
   c. the scribes
   d. the elders of the people
4. some of the chief priests

From the Upper Room to the Temple

It was Caiaphas, the high priest, along with the chief priests and the elders of the people who had first set out to accomplish Jesus' death (Matt. 26:3-4). Later when they gave Judas his money it was the chief priests and captain of the temple who were present (Luke 22:4). Thus these were the men Judas sought out to tell where to find Jesus. The logical place to find them would have been the temple and that was Judas's first stop. That would involve crossing Jerusalem and would take approximately twenty minutes. The captain of the temple, who was the ranking chief priest, would have been there, as would have some of the other chief priests. It is possible, also, that he found there some of the scribes, Pharisees, and elders of the people.

The writers indicate that, aside from some of the chief priests, these men did not accompany Judas themselves but rather sent some of the lesser "officials" to accomplish the task. No doubt they considered themselves above the actual deed, although they were perfectly willing to have others do it for them. The gathering of these men and the appointing of some officials to accompany Judas would have taken an additional fifteen to twenty minutes.

This group, however, had no legal authority over Jesus and evidently felt they should have soldiers with them to handle any possible resistance on the part of Jesus' supporters. Getting soldiers to go on a mission like this at night was not simply a matter of requesting them. Pilate was in Jerusalem to oversee personally the handling of any trouble that might start during the Feast. Additional soldiers brought in to handle crowd control would have been strategically assigned around the city. It would take Pilate himself to release some of these soldiers to assist in Jesus' arrest. Getting Pilate's permission was a problem in itself which they decided to take to the high priest.

From the Temple to Caiaphas

To get the assistance of Caiaphas required another trip across Jerusalem, for the palace of the high priest was in the same section of the city as the location of the upper room. Another half hour would be consumed in the trip and talking with Caiaphas. Caiaphas evidently felt that in order to be sure of getting Pilate to cooperate, they should solicit the help of Annas. Annas was the father-in-law of Caiaphas and had himself served as high priest, as had four of his sons. Later, one of his grandsons would also hold the office.

Annas was without a doubt one of the most powerful and influential men in Jerusalem. We can be sure it was Annas who received the cooperation of Pilate because the soldiers delivered Jesus to Annas following his arrest. This was, no doubt, where Pilate had told them to take him. He would not have instructed them to do so unless Annas himself had requested it.

From Caiaphas to Annas

Annas lived in the same section of the city as did Caiaphas, so the trip should not have taken more than ten minutes or so. It would have been after ten o'clock when the group arrived at Annas' house. Among the group was a servant of the high priest named Malchus. Since Caiaphas was the high priest and Annas still carried the honorary title, it is impossible to know which of the two men the servant represented. It is reasonable to assume, however, that he represented Annas since he was probably the one who carried the official request for soldiers from Annas to Pilate. Having received the necessary assistance from Annas, the group would then have gone back across Jerusalem to get to the fortress of Antonia.

Agony in the Garden

Kidron Valley

Prelude to Glory

From Annas to Pilate

Pilate made the fortress of Antonia his personal residence when in Jerusalem. It must have been nearly eleven o'clock when the group finally arrived at the fortress. More than likely, Pilate and his wife were in their personal quarters by this time. At any rate, Pilate's wife seems to have been aware of the goings-on as evidenced by her dream that night and her admonition the next morning. Both of these matters will be discussed in a later chapter, but suffice it to say for now that definitely Pilate and more than likely his wife were involved prior to the arrest of Jesus.

Since becoming governor, Pilate had had several disagreements with the Jewish leaders which had left relations strained between them. The exact nature of these disagreements will be discussed in Chapter Six, but for the moment it is important to understand that Pilate had a vested interest in complying with this late-night request from Annas. Besides, future benefit could be gained from the personal favor. This attitude would cause him trouble the next morning when the Jews threatened to complain to Caesar if they were not granted the crucifixion of Jesus. For the time being, however, Pilate was willing to grant the request. The band was complete and they had a contingent of soldiers to assist them in their appointed task. Judas then led the group to the last place he had known Jesus to be.

From Pilate to the Upper Room

Because this entailed another trip across Jerusalem, it must have been at least eleven-thirty when the soldiers knocked at the door of Mark's house. Mark tells of a young man who was in the Garden of Gethsemane wearing just a sheet when Jesus was arrested. Most scholars feel this young man was Mark himself and the reason for his being there dressed in that fashion was that he had been aroused from his sleep by the soldiers and, without taking time to dress, ran to warn Jesus. This and the fact that Judas had no way of knowing Jesus had left Mark's house are compelling reasons to believe they looked for Jesus at the upper room before going to the garden. Having missed Jesus at Mark's house, Judas led the band to the Garden of Gethsemane, the only other place he knew Jesus was accustomed to using.

Agony in the Garden

From the Upper Room to the Garden

Judas had the same choice of routes to Gethsemane as Jesus. Either route would require a trip across or around the city. Either way, from his vantage point on the side of the Mount of Olives, Jesus would see the torches long before they arrived at Gethsemane. Sometime after midnight Judas Iscariot would arrive to complete the betrayal he had denied only three hours earlier as he sat at supper with the apostles. From the Mount of Olives Jesus watched as the group slowly crossed the Kidron Valley and began their ascent up the side of the mount.

The Arrest

John 18:2 Now Judas, who betrayed him, knew the place, because Jesus had often met there with his disciples.

3 So Judas came to the grove, guiding a detachment of soldiers and some officials from the chief priests and Pharisees. They were carrying torches, lanterns and weapons.

Mark 14:42 [Jesus said] "Rise! Let us go! Here comes my betrayer!" (Matt. 26:46)

43 Just as he was speaking, Judas, one of the twelve appeared. With him was a crowd armed with swords and clubs, sent from the chief priests, the teachers of the law, and the elders. (Matt. 26:47; Luke 22:47)

44 Now the betrayer had arranged a signal with them: "The one I kiss is the man; arrest him and lead him away under guard." (Matt. 26:48)

45 Going at once to Jesus, Judas said, "Rabbi!" and kissed him. (Matt. 26:49; Luke 22:47)

Luke 22:48 But Jesus asked him, "Judas, are you betraying the Son of Man with a kiss?"

49 When Jesus' followers saw what was going to happen, they said, "Lord, should we strike with our swords?"

John 18:10 Then Simon Peter, who had a sword, drew it and

Prelude to Glory

	struck the high priest's servant, cutting off his right ear. (The servant's name was Malchus.) (Matt. 26:51; Mark 14:47; Luke 22:50)
Luke 22:51	But Jesus answered, "No more of this!" And he touched the man's ear and healed him.
John 18:11	Jesus commanded Peter, "Put your sword away! Shall I not drink the cup the Father has given me?"
Matt. 26:52	"Put your sword back in its place," Jesus said to him, "for all who draw the sword will die by the sword.
53	Do you think I cannot call on my Father, and he will at once put at my disposal more than twelve legions of angels?
54	But how then would the Scriptures be fulfilled that say it must happen in this way?"

Several things can be learned from this section of scripture. First and foremost is that Jesus was still in control. He had declined the opportunity to escape and now had forbidden his followers to fight in his behalf. Peter managed to get in one blow before Jesus stopped him, but Jesus quickly repaired the damage.

Jesus here attested to his own divinity. He stated clearly that he had the ability to call down twelve thousand angels from heaven if he wanted. It is interesting to notice that when the proper time came it took only one angel to overcome those who had been sent to guard the tomb. No doubt one would have been more than sufficient on this occasion also, but Jesus was making a statement concerning his divinity rather than an estimation of the amount of help he needed.

The important thing in Jesus' mind was that the scriptures be fulfilled. Jesus would later tell Pilate it was for this purpose he had been born. He did not want to suffer the pain and humiliation of the cross but this was the cup that had been assigned to him and he would not refrain from drinking it. He had asked that God remove it but that was not to be.

Jesus Disables His Captors

John 18:4	Jesus, knowing all that was going to happen to him, went out and asked them, "Who is it you want?"

Agony in the Garden

> 5 "Jesus of Nazareth," they replied. "I am he," Jesus said. (And Judas the traitor was standing there with them.)
> 6 When Jesus said, "I am he," they drew back and fell to the ground.

This scripture is one of the best kept secrets in the Bible. Jesus had been standing just inside the entrance to the garden with his disciples when Judas arrived. Judas had come forward and identified him for the soldiers with a kiss. Jesus then went out to where the soldiers were standing and asked them the simple question, "Who do you want?" Jesus was not seeking information with this question. He knew full well who it was they wanted. What he was establishing was a limit on whom they were going to get.

There was nothing in Jesus' reply that could be considered intimidating, but it is very possible there was something in his eyes. Jesus' eyes were able to cure a lame hand (Matt. 12:13). What the money changers in the temple saw when they looked into them was one thing (Matt. 21:12), but what the prostitute saw was quite another (John 8:11). Now, once again the eyes of Jesus seem to have a force all their own. If there could be any possible question of who was in control of the moment, it was answered beyond all doubt.

Rome's finest lay in the dirt at his feet with their faces to the ground. Alongside of them were Judas and the others who had come out thinking to take him by force. Having established who was in command, Jesus repeated his question to those then on the ground.

> **John 18:7** Again he asked them, "Who is it you want?" And they said, "Jesus of Nazareth."
> 8 "I told you that I am he," Jesus answered. "If you are looking for me, then let these men go."
> 9 This happened so that the words he had spoken would be fulfilled: "I have not lost one of those you gave me."

Prelude to Glory

Jesus Allows His Arrest

Jesus here established the ground rules under which he would go with them. They could take him and do with him as they must, but they could not take or harm any of his apostles. Meanwhile, Jesus made a further statement of general application.

Matt. 26:55 At that time Jesus said to the crowd, "Am I leading a rebellion, that you have come out with swords and clubs to capture me? Every day I sat in the temple courts teaching, and you did not arrest me. (Mark 14:48–49; Luke 22:52–53)
Luke 22:53 "But this is your hour—when darkness reigns."
Matt. 26:56 "But this has all taken place that the writings of the prophets might be fulfilled." Then all the disciples deserted him and fled. (Mark 14:49–50)

Jesus stood alone in the garden. The disciples had fled just as he had said they would. Jesus then allowed those who had come to arrest him to get up and complete their task.

Matt. 26:50 Jesus replied, "Friend, do what you came for." Then the men stepped forward, seized Jesus and arrested him. (Mark 14:46; John 18:12)

A Young Man in the Garden

One other event is recorded by Mark before the activities were completed.

Mark 14:51 A young man, wearing nothing but a linen garment, was following Jesus. When they seized him,
52 He fled naked, leaving his garment behind.

Mark was the only Gospel writer who recorded this event. None of the other Gospel writers were present when it took place. John and Matthew had already fled from the garden, and Luke was not there to begin with. It is easy to understand how the

Agony in the Garden

embarrassment of the situation would make such an impression on the young man that when he wrote his Gospel some thirty years later he would still have a vivid memory of the event.

Just as Moses lifted up the snake in the desert, so the Son of Man must be lifted up, that everyone who believes in him may have eternal life. For God so loved the world that he gave his one and only Son, that whoever believes in him shall not perish but have eternal life. For God did not send his Son into the world to condemn the world, but to save the world through him.

John 3:14–17

CHAPTER FIVE

A Jewish Inquisition

Two men came to the forefront following the arrest of Jesus. The first had the avowed purpose of seeing Jesus dead while the other did all that he could to prevent that death. The first was the Jewish high priest; the second was the Roman governor. In this chapter we will deal with the first of the two. Chapter Six will concern itself with the second.

The High Priest

Caiaphas must have felt his powerful position was threatened by the teachings of Jesus on the coming kingdom. He must have been well aware of the previous attempt by the people to make Jesus a king in the earthly sense. Although Jesus had no designs on his position, this did not dissuade Caiaphas from his avowed purpose.

Caiaphas had made his feelings perfectly clear a few days earlier while addressing a meeting of the Sanhedrin. It was just after Jesus had raised Lazarus from the dead and many people were beginning to follow him. John reports the statement which Caiaphas made before the Sanhedrin.

John 11:45 Therefore many of the Jews who had come to visit Mary, and had seen what Jesus did, put their faith in him.
46 But some of them went to the Pharisees and told them what Jesus had done.
47 Then the chief priests and the Pharisees called a meeting of the Sanhedrin. "What are we accomplishing?" they asked. "Here is this man performing many miraculous signs.

A Jewish Inquisition

> 48 If we let him go on like this, everyone will believe in him, and then the Romans will come and take away both our place and our nation."
>
> 49 Then one of them named Caiaphas, who was high priest that year, spoke up, "You know nothing at all!
>
> 50 You do not realize that it is better for you that one man die for the people than that the whole nation perish."

The chief priests and the Pharisees were concerned about the popularity Jesus was acquiring among the people. They appear to have visualized a situation in which they would be replaced as rulers by people selected by Jesus, should he become king. These Jews had a fear-hate relationship with the Romans. While they hated the oppression of Roman rule, they had managed to acquire for themselves relatively lucrative positions within the Roman system. They had reached an unspoken truce with the Romans; if they did not oppose Roman rule, they would be allowed a certain amount of independence in overseeing the religious aspect of the people's lives. This was a position of prestige which they were not anxious to relinquish. Additionally, they were afraid that if Jesus should acquire a large enough following the Romans might interpret this as a potentially rebellious situation. The use of Rome's military power could lead to the destruction of the nation. This fear was not entirely unjustified for just forty years later this very thing would happen as a result of the activities of the Zealots.

Caiaphas had his own position and prestige to be concerned about. To support his desire that the "Jesus threat" be eliminated by killing Jesus, he took this occasion to play upon the fears of the Sanhedrin. To rationalize his position he claimed that his concern was for the entire nation and that the death of one man was an acceptable price to pay for the life of that nation. This position worked to conceal his private selfish motives. John points out in verses 51 and 52 that, without knowing it, Caiaphas was in fact prophesying the fulfillment of Isaiah 49:6 which said:

> It is too small a thing for you to be my servant to restore the tribes of Jacob and bring back those of Israel I have kept. I will also make you a light for the Gentiles, that you may bring my salvation to the ends of the earth.

Having in this manner gained the support of the Sanhedrin, Caiaphas chose to remain in the background calling the shots. This would serve to ensure the continuation of his personal power and prestige while making it appear he was only looking after the physical and spiritual welfare of the people.

Judas has taken some blame over the years which by all rights should have rested at the feet of Caiaphas. Since there is no justification for what Judas did, he richly deserves his place of infamy in the history of the world. He was not alone, however, in deserving condemnation. Caiaphas deserved as much, if not more, than Judas. Judas was but a pawn in the game. Caiaphas was the prime mover and signal caller. From that time forward Caiaphas was able to use his position to further his selfish purpose without becoming personally involved. That purpose was consummated with the arrest of Jesus in the Garden of Gethsemane.

Caiaphas had his chance to see Jesus condemned before the night was over, but first he had to wait until Annas sent Jesus to him. The soldiers had been told by Pilate to deliver Jesus to Annas and that is what they did.

The Appearance before Annas

John 18:12 Then the detachment of soldiers with its commander and the Jewish officials arrested Jesus. They bound him
   13 And brought him first to Annas, who was the father-in-law of Caiaphas, the high priest that year.
   14 Caiaphas was the one who had advised the Jews that it would be good if one man died for the people.
   19 Meanwhile, the high priest questioned Jesus about his disciples and his teaching.
   20 "I have spoken openly to the world," Jesus replied. "I always taught in synagogues or at the temple, where all the Jews come together. I said nothing in secret.
   21 Why question me? Ask those who heard me. Surely they know what I said."

A Jewish Inquisition

22 When Jesus said this, one of the officials nearby struck him in the face. "Is that any way to answer the high priest?" he demanded.

23 "If I said something wrong," Jesus replied, "testify as to what is wrong. But if I spoke the truth, why did you strike me?"

24 Then Annas sent him, still bound, to Caiaphas the high priest.

The appearance before Annas was short and accomplished no meaningful purpose. The soldiers had been told to deliver him there and they had done so. The questions asked by Annas were strictly for show and Jesus refused to be a part of the charade. Annas knew perfectly well what Jesus had been teaching, but it was necessary to build a case of treason against Rome in order to get the sentence that Caiaphas wanted. The question about Jesus' disciples and his teachings was merely an attempt to incriminate him. Annas wanted these soldiers to be able to testify that Jesus had been questioned about his activities. Later they charged that his teachings had been subversive.

When he refused to accommodate Annas in this endeavor, Jesus was hit in the face by one of the Jewish officials. Having completed his charade and realizing he was going to get nowhere with his questions, Annas sent Jesus to Caiaphas. Caiaphas had already begun to assemble some of the members of the Sanhedrin who he knew would be sympathetic to his position. It was before this select group that Jesus was then taken.

Appearance before Caiaphas

Matt. 26:57 Those who had arrested Jesus took him to Caiaphas, the high priest, where the teachers of the law and the elders had assembled. (Mark 14:53; Luke 22:54)

John 18:15 Simon Peter and another disciple were following Jesus. Because this disciple was known to the high priest, he went with Jesus into the high priest's courtyard, (Matt. 26:58; Mark 14:54)

16 but Peter had to wait outside at the door. The other

Prelude to Glory

disciple, who was known to the high priest, came back, spoke to the girl on duty there and brought Peter in.

This passage strengthens the belief that John was well known among the rich and influential in Jerusalem. It also lends credibility to the belief that John may have had a personal residence in this part of the city which will become a factor when we consider the early morning visits to the tomb on Sunday. It also provides Peter with his first opportunity to deny Jesus.

The First Denial—At the Gate

At the Last Supper Jesus had predicted Peter would deny him three times before the cock crowed the next morning. The Gospel writers indicate Peter probably denied him at least four times before the night was over and possibly even more. The fact that Peter may have denied Jesus more than three times should cause

Palace of the High Priest

A Jewish Inquisition

us no concern; all it proves is that Jesus was being generous in his prediction. There is certainly no doubt that Peter denied him at least three times just as Jesus had said he would.

When John told the maid on duty at the gate that Peter was with him it was only natural she would respond by asking Peter if he, too, was one of Jesus' disciples.

> **John 18:17** "Surely you are not one of this man's disciples?" the girl at the door asked Peter. He replied, "I am not."
> **18** It was cold, and the servants and officials stood around a fire they had made to keep warm. Peter also was standing with them, warming himself. (Luke 22:55)

The palace of the high priest was in the southwestern section of Jerusalem. It was probably not far from the upper room, Herod's palace, and Annas' house where Jesus had first been taken. Before Jesus arrived, perhaps even before he was arrested, select members of the Sanhedrin had been gathered in anticipation of an opportunity to find something with which to charge him before Pilate. We do not know how long Jesus was held here, but it was at least one hour (Luke 22:59) and possibly as long as four hours. Two things seem to account for the length of time spent here. First, time was needed to find witnesses who could agree with each other, and second, they had to wait until daybreak to begin the formal trial before the Sanhedrin. Meanwhile Peter seems to have remained by the fire for some period of time before he was recognized as one who had been with Jesus.

The Second Denial—by the Fire

> **Luke 22:56** A servant girl saw him seated there in the firelight. She looked closely at him and said, "This man was with him." (Matt. 26:69; Mark 14:66–67; John 18:25)
> **Mark 14:68** But he denied it. "I don't know or understand what you're talking about," he said, and went out into the entryway. (Matt. 26:70; Luke 22:57)

Prelude to Glory

The palace of the high priest is believed to have had two large courtyards within the walls. It was in one of these that the soldiers had built a fire to keep warm. They had delivered Jesus to Caiaphas as directed by Annas then retired to the courtyard to wait for further instructions. The fire had already been built when Peter arrived and he took advantage of it as he waited for John who had evidently gone inside to see what was happening with Jesus. When Peter realized that the light of the fire allowed the maid and others to recognize him he moved away to find a more secluded spot to wait. The entryway or covered porch which surrounded the building provided an excellent place which would have been both out of the way and relatively dark. Here Peter continued his wait, but not without once again being confronted by another maid who recognized him.

The Third Denial—on the Porch

> **Matt. 26:71** Then he went out to the gateway, where another girl saw him and said to the people there, "This fellow was with Jesus of Nazareth." (Mark 14:69; Luke 22:58)
> 72 He denied it again, with an oath: "I don't know the man!"

It appears to have been at about this time that the questioning of Jesus got underway inside the palace. Caiaphas was well in control of the situation, as far as directing the Jews' thinking was concerned. It is important to be aware of the fact that this was a handpicked group, not the entire Sanhedrin. Also, this was an inquiry, not a trial. In fact, Jewish law prohibited a trial from being conducted at night. What was happening here was that Caiaphas was laying the groundwork for the charges that would be brought against Jesus when they were able to convene the Sanhedrin for a formal trial after daybreak.

Caiaphas had two problems to overcome in order to get Jesus sentenced to death. The first was the Sanhedrin. There he either had to bring charges which could be supported by witnesses or get Jesus to confess, in which case witnesses would not be necessary. The second problem was to find charges which would

A Jewish Inquisition

be accepted by Pilate, who was the only one who could pronounce the death sentence.

Israel's legal system was very advanced for its day. This was because the system, in its original form, had been given to the Israelites by God. They had distorted it as they had distorted most other things since the death of Moses, but, even so, it was still far superior to most other systems and was replete with safeguards for the accused. Even though some of these safeguards were ignored in Jesus' case, it was still necessary to try him for some punishable offense and to do so in a manner relatively consistent with Jewish law. An effort was made, therefore, to find someone who had witnessed Jesus doing or saying something that violated the law.

Sometime in the early morning hours after Caiaphas gathered his cohorts and witnesses together, Jesus was brought into their midst to be questioned and, if possible, tricked into an incriminating admission.

Matt. 26:59	The chief priests and the whole Sanhedrin were looking for false evidence against Jesus so that they could put him to death. (Mark 14:55)
60	But they did not find any, though many false witnesses came forward. (Mark 14:56)
Mark 14:57	Then some stood up and gave this false testimony against him:
58	"We heard him say, 'I will destroy this man-made temple and in three days will build another, not made by man.'"
59	Yet even then their testimony did not agree
Matt. 26:60	Finally two came forward
61	and declared, "This fellow said, 'I am able to destroy the temple of God and rebuild it in three days.'"
Mark 14:60	Then the high priest stood up before them and asked Jesus, "Are you not going to answer? What is this testimony that these men are bringing against you?" (Matt. 26:62)
61	But Jesus remained silent and gave no answer. Again the high priest asked him, "Are you the

Prelude to Glory

	Christ, the Son of the Blessed One?" (Matt. 26:63)
62	"I am," said Jesus "And you will see the Son of Man sitting at the right hand of the Mighty One and coming on the clouds of heaven." (Matt. 26:64)
63	The high priest tore his clothes. "Why do we need any more witnesses?" he asked. (Matt. 26:65)
64	"You have heard the blasphemy. What do you think?" They all condemned him as worthy of death. (Matt. 26:66)
Luke 22:63	The men who were guarding Jesus began mocking and beating him.
Matt. 26:67	Then they spit in his face and struck him with their fists. Others slapped him. (Mark 14:65)
Luke 22:64	They blindfolded him and demanded, "Prophesy! Who hit you?" (Matt. 26:68; Mark 14:65)
65	And they said many other insulting things to him.

This was a questioning of Jesus by the high priest in the presence of certain of his cohorts for the purpose of coming up with charges that could be brought before the Sanhedrin. To make these charges they brought in false witnesses to see if they could find enough evidence to ensure a conviction. Evidently this was not a very easy task as it seems they listened to a number of witnesses before finding two whose testimony they felt would stand up. The charge that was finally decided upon was blasphemy, which under Jewish law did carry the death penalty. Just before dawn Jesus was taken from the palace of the high priest to the temple where he would be brought before the Sanhedrin. As Jesus was being led out through the courtyard another attempt was made to associate Peter with him.

The Fourth Denial—One Hour Later

Luke 22:59	About an hour later another [one of the high priest's servants, a relative of the man whose ear Peter had cut off] asserted, "Certainly this fellow was with him, for he is a Galilean." (Matt. 26:73; Mark 14:70; John 18:26)

A Jewish Inquisition

Matt. 26:74 Then he began to call down curses on himself and he swore to them, "I don't know the man!" Immediately a rooster crowed. (Mark 14:71–72; Luke 22:60; John 18:27)
Luke 22:61 The Lord turned and looked straight at Peter. Then Peter remembered the word the Lord had spoken to him: "Before the rooster crows today, you will disown me three times." (Matt. 26:75; Mark 14:72)
62 And he went outside and wept bitterly.

Trial by the Sanhedrin

The Great Sanhedrin was the highest judicial tribunal of the Jewish nation. Under the Maccabees it had held the power of life and death. The Romans, however, removed the power to award the death sentence. Although the Great Sanhedrin could try capital cases and often did so, the death sentence, if awarded had to be ratified by the Roman governor.

The Great Sanhedrin was located in Jerusalem and was comprised of seventy-one members. Other Sanhedrins in the outlying provinces were composed of twenty-three members (judges). Each city having two hundred thirty men was allowed to have a Sanhedrin. Cases tried by the lesser Sanhedrins could be appealed to the Great Sanhedrin. From the Great Sanhedrin there was no appeal.

The members of the Sanhedrin were chosen from the chief priests, elders, and scribes. It was necessary to have priests and scribes in the body, and they were usually quite numerous, though the majority of the members are thought to have been laymen. The relative numbers of the three classes are not definitely known. The Pharisees and the Sadducees were both represented, sometimes one and sometimes the other being in the majority. Most of the scribes probably belonged to the Pharisees.

Great care was taken in the selection of members, who were required to be "morally and physically blameless." They were also expected to be learned in law, sciences, and languages. It was necessary for them to have been judges in their native towns; to have been transferred from there to the small Sanhedrin, which met at the temple mount; and thence to the second small Sanhedrin, which met at the entrance of the temple hall. They were not eligible unless they were the fathers of families, in order that they might be able to sympathize when cases involving domestic affairs were brought before them.

The Sanhedrin held daily sessions, lasting from the close of the morning sacrifice to the commencement of the evening sacrifice. On Sabbaths and festival days, however, they held no sessions.

It was the Great Sanhedrin before which Jesus was brought for trial. It is not known exactly where the official meeting place of the Sanhedrin was at the time Jesus was brought before it. One place which had been the official meeting place was the "chamber of hewn stones" in the southwest corner of the Court of Women at the temple. The context makes it very likely that this is where Jesus was tried, but there is no way of knowing for sure.

As President of the Sanhedrin, Caiaphas was in an excellent position to direct the thinking of the group that morning. However, there were members of the Sanhedrin who were disciples of Jesus and would not have allowed a travesty of justice to take place. Principal among these were Nicodemus (John 3:1) and Joseph of Arimathea (Mark 15:43). The presence of twenty-three of the seventy-one members was required to make a quorum. Without a doubt Caiaphas carefully selected the twenty-three. None of Jesus' supporters were present when the trial was convened just after sunrise (Luke 23:51). Concerning a capital trial before the Sanhedrin the Mishnah states:

> In capital cases they hold the trial during the daytime and the verdict must also be during the daytime. . . . In capital cases a verdict of acquittal may be reached on the same day, but a verdict of conviction not until the following day. . . . Trials may not be held on a Sabbath or Feast day, or on the eve of a Sabbath or Feast day. (Mish., Sanhedrin 4.1)

Luke 22:66 At daybreak the council of the elders of the people, both the chief priests and teachers of the law, met together, and Jesus was led before them. (Matt. 27:1; Mark 15:1)

A Jewish Inquisition

> 67 "If you are the Christ," they said, "Tell us." Jesus answered, "If I tell you, you will not believe me,
> 68 And if I asked you, you would not answer.
> 69 But from now on, the Son of Man will be seated at the right hand of the mighty God."
> 70 They all asked, "Are you then the Son of God?" He replied, "You are right in saying I am."
> 71 Then they said, "Why do we need any more testimony? We have heard it from his own lips."

Most of the rules for trial were observed in this case with the exception of announcing a guilty verdict on the same day as the trial. In Jerusalem the Sabbath and Feast day eve restrictions did not come into effect until the ninth hour (3:00 P.M.). Therefore, since the trial was completed in the morning on the fourteenth it was legal. Had it been on the fifteenth, which was the Feast day itself, it would have been illegal.

While a delegation of council members was in the process of taking Jesus from the council chamber to the fortress of Antonia to have the sentence ratified by Pilate, a lone figure was making his way through the streets of Jerusalem on his way to a deserted place outside the walls of the city.

The Suicide of Judas

Judas Iscariot had been following the proceedings of the night with more than casual interest. He had betrayed Jesus, but it does not appear he believed that in doing so he was delivering Jesus to his death. As the night wore on, however, it became more and more apparent that this indeed would be the final result of his actions. If he had any lingering doubts as to the ultimate outcome, they were removed when the Sanhedrin voted to deliver Jesus to Pilate for execution.

> **Matt. 27:1** Early in the morning, all the chief priests and the elders of the people came to the decision to put Jesus to death.
> 2 They bound him, led him away and handed him over to Pilate, the governor.

3   When Judas, who had betrayed him, saw that Jesus was condemned, he was seized with remorse and returned the thirty silver coins to the chief priests and the elders.
4   "I have sinned," he said, "for I have betrayed innocent blood." "What is that to us?" they replied. "That's your responsibility."
5   So Judas threw the money into the temple and left. Then he went away and hanged himself.
6   The chief priests picked up the coins and said, "It is against the law to put this into the treasury, since it is blood money."
7   So they decided to use the money to buy the potter's field as a burial place for foreigners.
8   That is why it has been called the Field of Blood to this day. (Acts 1:19)
9   Then what was spoken by Jeremiah the prophet was fulfilled: "They took the thirty silver coins, the price set on him by the people of Israel.
10 And they used them to buy the potter's field, as the Lord commanded me." (Zech. 11:13; Jer. 18:2; 19:12; 32:6–15)

Some have considered this account of the suicide of Judas to be contradicted by Acts 1:18 which states ". . . he fell headlong, his body burst open and all his intestines spilled out." There is, however, no contradiction between these two accounts when the ensuing events are considered.

Judas found a desolate location somewhere in the wilderness outside Jerusalem where he hanged himself. This would have been sometime on Thursday morning. The body would hang there in the sun until it was accidentally discovered. Two to three days would have been sufficient for the body to decompose to the extent that should it drop from any height at all it would "burst open."

Early on Sunday morning there was a violent earthquake associated with the resurrection of Jesus. This earthquake would have been more than sufficient to cause the body to drop from wherever it was hanging. The result of a decomposing body's

A Jewish Inquisition

falling from a tree or cliff from which it had hung would produce exactly the results described in Acts.

While the Son of God hung from the cross of Calvary for the sins of mankind, the son of perdition hung in a deserted place, the victim of his own greed.

Caiaphas, in the meantime, did not go to the fortress of Antonia with the others. This would have been beneath the dignity of the office of high priest. Others were left to complete the task which he had begun. To this end we find the delegation of chief priests and elders present at all of the ensuing events right up to and including the crucifixion.

This then is how Caiaphas, the high priest of the nation of Israel, engineered the events from beginning to end to achieve the death of Jesus of Nazareth, "a man accredited by God . . . by miracles, wonders, and signs" (Acts 2:22).

* * * * *

Woe to you, teachers of the law and Pharisees, you hypocrites! You build tombs for the prophets and decorate the graves of the righteous. And you say, "If we had lived in the days of our forefathers, we would not have taken part with them in shedding the blood of the prophets." So you testify against yourselves that you are the descendants of those who murdered the prophets. Fill up, then, the measure of the sin of your forefathers!

Matthew 23:29–32

CHAPTER SIX

Trial of a King

In Chapter Five the leading character was Caiaphas, the high priest. Through various legal maneuvers he had managed to have Jesus condemned to death by the Sanhedrin for the crime of blasphemy. Now it was necessary to have the sentence ratified by the Roman governor. This posed a problem in itself inasmuch as blasphemy was not a crime as far as Rome was concerned. It was necessary to find something else with which to charge Jesus before Pilate.

The Romans practiced emperor worship and therein the Jews found the law under which they could charge Jesus. If they could show that Jesus was in fact attempting to set up a kingdom of his own and was trying to get Roman subjects to switch their allegiance, they would then have produced an offense punishable by death under the Roman system. It is not clear if this charge was thought up while they were before Pilate or if it had been planned ahead of time.

Only the delegation from the Sanhedrin and the Roman soldiers took Jesus before Pilate. The soldiers had been present all night long and the delegation from the Sanhedrin would have been necessary to bring the official verdict to Pilate. In all probability there were no more than twenty or twenty-five persons, including the soldiers, in the group that escorted Jesus to Pilate. The trip from the Sanhedrin's meeting room in the temple through the underground passageway and into the fortress would not have taken more than five or ten minutes.

The Hour of the First Trial

The time of day that Jesus stood before Pilate has been a source of controversy inasmuch as there appears to be a difference between John's Gospel and Mark's. Reconciling the two is not difficult when we understand that Rome and Jerusalem had two

Trial of a King

The Lithostrotos (Pavement)

different time systems. The Jews viewed the day as a twelve-hour period and the night as a separate twelve-hour period (John 11:9–10).

The Jewish night began at 6:00 P.M. and ended at 6:00 A.M. It was divided into four watches of three hours each, the first watch being from 6:00 P.M. to 9:00 P.M.; the second, from 9:00 P.M. to 12:00 midnight; the third, from midnight to 3:00 A.M.; and the fourth, from 3:00 A.M. to 6:00 A.M. The Jews originally had three night watches of four hours each but following the Roman conquest in 63 B.C. they adopted the Roman system of four watches of three hours each. When Matthew wrote that Jesus walked on the water to the disciples during the fourth watch (14:25), he was designating the time as being between 3:00 A.M. and 6:00 A.M.

The Jewish day ran from 6:00 A.M. to 6:00 P.M. and was divided into twelve hours. Mark says it was the "third hour" (Mark 15:25) when Jesus was placed on the cross. This would have been 9:00 A.M.

Thus, the nights were divided into four watches and the days were divided into twelve hours. The Jewish day always began at sunrise and ended at sunset, and the length of each hour varied according to the time of year. The maximum time from sunrise to sunset in that latitude is fourteen hours and twelve minutes while the minimum is nine hours and forty-eight minutes. This makes a difference of four hours and twenty-four minutes between the longest and the shortest days of the year. If each were divided into twelve equal parts, there would be a difference of twenty-two minutes between the longest and shortest hours of the year, with the actual length of an hour varying from forty-nine minutes to seventy-one.

The first hour began at sunrise, the sixth hour ended at noon, and the twelfth ended at sunset. The third hour equally divided the period between sunrise and noon, while the ninth hour divided the period between noon and sunset. This is the Jewish time system that was in effect during Jesus' life. The Synoptic writers used this system of time.

Although they divided the night into four watches, the Romans still referred to the day as a twenty-four hour period beginning at midnight. Thus, under the Roman system 6:00 A.M. was referred to as the sixth hour.

Trial of a King

The Synoptic writers all wrote their Gospels prior to the destruction of Jerusalem, and all three appear to have used the Jewish system of reporting times. John, on the other hand, is believed to have written his Gospel, twenty-five to thirty years after the destruction and definitely used the Roman system of time. This is why John could say that Jesus went before Pilate at "about the sixth hour" (6:00 P.M.) (19:14) and Mark could report that Jesus was crucified at the "third hour" (9:00 P.M.) (15:25) without there being any contradiction between the two.

Finally, with regard to the time of day when Jesus was brought before Pilate it appears from John's report that it was the sixth hour when Jesus was sentenced by Pilate. There is no doubt that the sentence was handed down by Pilate much later than 6:00 A.M. We know that Jesus was not taken before the Sanhedrin until after daybreak (Luke 22:66) nor could he have been under Jewish law. Too many things transpired between the appearance before the Sanhedrin and the sentencing by Pilate for them all to have been completed by 6:00 A.M. The trip to Herod's palace and back to the fortress would have taken a minimum of an hour. At least another thirty minutes would have been consumed while Jesus was taken into the fortress and scourged. Additional time was consumed by Pilate's questioning of Jesus and his accusers, not to mention the time consumed when the multitude arrived to ask for the release of a prisoner. It could not have been much before 8:00 A.M. when Pilate finally pronounced sentence.

John reports both trials before Pilate as if they were one occasion. He does not mention the fact of the intervening trip to be questioned by Herod. John reports the events before Pilate and states that it was the "sixth hour" when these things took place. John is obviously referring to the time when the events before Pilate began, not when Pilate pronounced sentence. Thus, when Jesus was first taken before Pilate it was about 6:00 A.M. This would have been possible if the trial before the Sanhedrin had begun around 5:30 A.M.

The Roman Governor

Pontius Pilate had been governor of the province of Judea for about four years when Jesus was brought before him. They had

Caesarea—Ancient Roman Capital

Aquaduct to Caesarea

been troublesome years both for him and for the Jews. The Roman governors were not popular to begin with and Pilate had managed to offend the Jewish leaders in additional ways on two separate occasions. Josephus reports that the first event took place in Caesarea when some of the Jews came there to protest against Roman ensigns being brought into Jerusalem (Wars II, IX, 2–3). A short while later, according to Josephus, he again offended them by taking money from the temple treasury to build aqueducts. This second disturbance culminated in the slaughter of a number of Jews (Wars II, IX, 4). These two events resulted in Pilate's being put on semi-probation by the authorities in Rome who disliked unrest in the provinces. Six years later he was removed from office because of continued mishandling of his authority. For the time being, he was attempting to appease these leaders while striving to maintain absolute authority over the people. This proved to be a major problem when Jesus was brought before him.

It is impossible to read the account of the trials before Pilate without realizing that Pilate did not want to have Jesus crucified. This is actually very difficult to understand. Pilate was known as a blood-thirsty individual, who had not hesitated to have hundreds slaughtered in the streets of Caesarea. He had been promoted to governor following a military career and certainly had no aversion to killing or having someone killed. Yet, in the case of Jesus, he did everything in his power to prevent the crucifixion. He obviously saw through the Jewish charade, yet was too weak in character to use his authority to prevent Caiaphas from murdering the Messiah.

Whatever the case, Pilate became the main character in the "trial scene" as the drama continued to unfold. No matter how hard he tried, he could not avoid his date with destiny. Even though he believed Jesus to be innocent, with all his authority he could not bring himself to put an end to the travesty.

The First Trial before Pilate

Luke 23:1 Then the whole assembly rose and led him off to Pilate. (Matt. 27:2; Mark 15:1)
John 18:28 Then the Jews led Jesus from Caiaphas to the

palace of the Roman governor. By now it was early morning, and to avoid ceremonial uncleanness the Jews did not enter the palace; they wanted to be able to eat the Passover.

According to Numbers 9:6–14, those who were ceremonially unclean at the time of the Passover would have to wait until the second Passover which would not come until a month later. It is not clear what type of uncleanness would have been incurred by entering the fortress. One possibility is the mere fact that this was a gentile or heathen fortress. Another possibility is that entering the fortress meant contact with a dead body. Even entering the house where a dead body lay could cause a person to become defiled. Once defiled in this manner, a person would remain unclean for seven days (Num. 9:6; 19:14). Prisoners dying under the various forms of maltreatment inflicted upon them in this Roman garrison was not uncommon. This being the case, the probability of a dead body's being within the confines that morning was more than these Jews were willing to risk.

Additional light is shed on the defilement, which the Jews believed attached itself to the fortress, by Josephus, who writes:

> When Herod [the Great] became king he rebuilt this tower, which was very conveniently situated, in a magnificent manner; and because he was a friend to Antonius [Mark Antony], he called it by the name of Antonia and as he found these vestments lying there, he retained them in the same place, as believing that, while he had them in his custody, the people would make no innovations against him. . . . the Romans, when they entered the government, took possession of these vestments of the high priest . . . and seven days before a festival they were delivered to him by the captain of the guard. When the high priest had purified them for *seven days*, and made use of them, they were laid up again in the same chamber where they had been laid up before, and this the very next day after the feast was over. (Ant. XVIII, IV, 3, italics added)

If the garments were considered unclean for a period of seven days after being in the fortress, so would be any person who went within the confines of Antonia.

Trial of a King

The Jews came as near to the fortress as they dared, then let the soldiers take Jesus the rest of the way into the fortress. No doubt they remained in the underground passageway between the temple and the fortress. Jesus, meanwhile, had been taken into the fortress to an area referred to as the "pavement" which was an open courtyard located between the arches. Since the Jewish leaders would not come into the fortress, it was necessary for Pilate to go to where they were.

> **John 18:29** So Pilate came out to them and asked, "What charges are you bringing against this man?"
> **30** "If he were not a criminal," they replied, "we would not have handed him over to you."
> **Luke 23:2a** And they began to accuse him, saying, "We have found this man subverting our nation."

Pilate's First Attempt to Save Jesus

> **John 18:31** Pilate said, "Take him yourselves and judge him by your own law." "But we have no right to execute anyone," the Jews objected.
> **32** This happened so that the words Jesus had spoken indicating the kind of death he was going to die would be fulfilled. (See John 12:32.)

Pilate first attempted to save Jesus by claiming he did not have jurisdiction in the matter. He wanted to put the matter back into their hands, knowing they could find Jesus guilty if they wanted but could not put him to death. The Jews, however, would have none of it. They immediately brought up the next charge, which they knew Pilate would be forced to investigate.

> **Luke 23:2b** "He opposes payment of taxes to Caesar and claims to be Christ, a king."

This charge was one which was punishable under Roman law so Pilate went back inside the fortress to question Jesus.

> **John 18:33** Pilate then went back inside the palace, sum-

moned Jesus and asked him, "Are you the king of the Jews?" (Matt. 27:11; Mark 15:2; Luke 23:3)

34 "Is that your own idea," Jesus asked, "or did others talk to you about me?"

35 "Do you think I am a Jew?" Pilate replied. "It was your people and your chief priests who handed you over to me. What is it you have done?"

36 Jesus said, "My kingdom is not of this world. If it were, my servants would fight to prevent my arrest by the Jews. But now my kingdom is from another place."

37 "You are a king, then!" said Pilate. Jesus answered, "You are right in saying I am a king. In fact, for this reason I was born, and for this I came into the world, to testify to the truth. Everyone on the side of truth listens to me."

38a "What is truth?" Pilate asked.

Pilate's Second Attempt to Save Jesus

This short conversation convinced Pilate that Jesus had no desire to rebel against the Roman empire and establish his own kingdom. Pilate obviously did not understand the full import of what Jesus was saying but neither did he deem him to be a threat to Rome. Therefore, he would let him go.

John 18:38b With this he went out again to the Jews and said, "I find no basis for a charge against him." (Luke 23:4)

Luke 23:5 But they insisted, "He stirs up the people all over Judea by his teaching. He started in Galilee and has come all the way here."

Pilate's Third Attempt to Save Jesus

Pilate tried to send Jesus back to the Jews for trial but they would not have it. He then questioned Jesus and determined there was no basis for criminal charges. Neither of these attempts to free Jesus had succeeded, but now Pilate believed he had found a means by which to rid himself of the problem. Galilee was in Herod's jurisdiction and he knew Herod was in Jerusalem for the Passover.

> **Luke 23:6** On hearing this, Pilate asked if the man was a Galilean.
> 7 When he learned that Jesus was under Herod's jurisdiction, he sent him to Herod, who was also in Jerusalem at that time.

The Trial before Herod

The Herod before whom Jesus was taken was Herod Antipas. Herod was too busy with the enjoyment of being king to have time to assume any of the responsibilities of that position. His life can be summed up as one of self-indulgence and debauchery. He had become so excited watching his stepdaughter dance that he was willing to have John the Baptist beheaded to gain additional favors from her (Matt. 14:6–9). Josephus reports that Herod, in order to build his capital city of Tiberius on the Sea of Galilee, had "many sepulchres" taken away. The result was that anyone entering the city was considered unclean for a period of seven days. (Ant. XVIII, II, 3). This did not bother Herod, who proceeded to populate his new capital by giving free land and houses to those who would live there.

The trial before Herod took place between six and seven o'clock and lasted only a few minutes. Herod wanted to be entertained and Jesus had no intention of accommodating him.

> **Luke 23:8** When Herod saw Jesus, he was greatly pleased, because for a long time he had been wanting to see him. From what he had heard about him, he hoped to see him perform some miracle.
> 9 He plied him with many questions, but Jesus gave him no answer.
> 10 The chief priests and the teachers of the law were standing there, vehemently accusing him.
> 11 Then Herod and his soldiers ridiculed and

Prelude to Glory

> mocked him. Dressing him in an elegant robe, they sent him back to Pilate.
> 12 That day Herod and Pilate became friends—before this they had been enemies.

Herod only agreed to see Jesus in order to enjoy some early morning entertainment. Dressing Jesus in royal garments and mocking him gave Herod and the soldiers some short-lived entertainment, but that was the extent of what they were able to accomplish. Herod soon tired of the game and sent him back to Pilate.

Luke says that Herod and Pilate became friends from that time on. We don't know the source of the animosity that had existed between these two, but it very possibly had to do with the fact that Herod's brother, Archelaus, had been removed from his throne and replaced by Roman procurators. It would be somewhat natural for Herod to resent someone who now governed in place of his brother. Perhaps Pilate's recognition of his jurisdiction eased Herod's resentment.

The Second Trial before Pilate

By seven-thirty the problem was back in Pilate's lap. The Jews were relentless in their quest to obtain the death of Jesus. For the time being, however, Pilate seemed determined to find some way of avoiding the inevitable. When Jesus was brought in to him a second time Pilate tried another tactic in his attempt to save him.

> **Mark 15:6** Now it was the custom at the Feast to release a prisoner whom the people requested.
> 7 A man called Barabbas was in prison with the insurrectionists who had committed murder in the uprising. (Matt. 27:15-16)

Pilate's Fourth Attempt to Save Jesus

> **Luke 23:13** Pilate called together the chief priests, and the rulers and the people,

Trial of a King

14 and said to them, "You brought me this man as one who was inciting the people to rebellion. I have examined him in your presence and have found no basis for your charges against him.

15 Neither has Herod, for he sent him back to us; as you can see, he has done nothing to deserve death."

John 18:39 "But it is your custom for me to release to you one prisoner at the time of the Passover. Do you want me to release the 'king of the Jews'?"

Matt. 27:17 So when the crowd had gathered, Pilate asked them, "Which one do you want me to release to you: Barabbas, or Jesus who is called Christ?"

18 For he knew it was out of envy that they had handed Jesus over to him.

This conversation was between Pilate and the accusers who had first brought Jesus to him. A similar conversation with a crowd which had gathered outside the front gate of the fortress took place later. Pilate here took a calculated risk. He knew that Jesus had done nothing wrong and could not be considered dangerous. By offering them the freedom of Barabbas, who would immediately become a plague on their society, he felt he would prompt them into selecting Jesus. Pilate misjudged the depth of their commitment to seeing Jesus dead.

Luke 23:18 With one voice they cried out, "Away with this man! Release Barabbas to us!"

19 (Barabbas had been thrown into prison for an insurrection in the city, and for murder.) (John 18:40)

The Arrival of the Multitude

About this time a crowd arrived outside the fortress to ask Pilate to give them a prisoner as was the custom. Many commentators have felt that there was a single conversation which took place between Pilate, Jesus' accusers, and the multitude concerning the release of Barabbas. Several facts, however, point to the probability that two different conversations took place regarding Barabbas.

The first conversation, as already indicated, was between Pilate and the accusers who had brought Jesus to him in the first place. In that conversation it was Pilate who first mentioned the name Barabbas. He did so to provide the accusers with what he believed would be an unacceptable alternative to releasing Jesus. The Jewish authorities, however, would have no part of it.

The second conversation took place between Pilate and the crowd that had gathered to seek the release of a prisoner. Many, if not most, of the prisoners in the fortress were being held for political reasons and were folk heroes whom the people would be glad to have in their midst again. It was political prisoners that Pilate was accustomed to releasing on these occasions.

The people could not have known that Jesus had been arrested. Indeed, the Jewish authorities had done their best to keep the people from finding out because they feared a riot would result (Mark 14:1–2). It is doubtful that more than a couple of hundred out of some one hundred thousand people in the city were actually aware of the trial and conviction. The majority were absorbed with the Passover festivities and totally unaware of what their leaders were doing.

Finally, the people would not have been allowed within the confines of the fortress. Since large crowds can be difficult to manage, there is no way Pilate would have allowed a large group to come within the fortress. The people would have been on the steps at the front of the fortress, while the accusers were more than likely still in the underground passageway. Pilate appears to have been going from one group to the other. Following the leaders' refusal to accept the release of Jesus, Pilate made the same offer to the people.

Pilate's Fifth Attempt to Save Jesus

Matt. 27:15 Now it was the governor's custom at the Feast to release a prisoner chosen by the crowd.
Mark 15:8 The crowd came up and asked Pilate to do for them what he usually did.
9 "Do you want me to release to you the king of the Jews?" asked Pilate,
10 knowing it was out of envy that the chief priests had handed Jesus over to him.

Trial of a King

Matt. 27:20 But the chief priests and the elders persuaded the crowd to ask for Barabbas and to have Jesus executed. (Mark 15:11)

The crowd would not have asked for Barabbas of their own accord. Mark tells us clearly the reason they, not Pilate, brought up the name Barabbas was that the chief priests had stirred them up. At this point mob psychology apparently took effect which the priests were able to manipulate to their own benefit.

Matt. 27:21 "Which of the two do you want me to release to you?" asked the governor. "Barabbas," they answered.
    22 "What shall I do, then, with Jesus who is called Christ?" Pilate asked. They all answered, "Crucify him!" (Mark 15:12–13)
    23 "Why? What crime has he committed?" asked Pilate. But they shouted all the louder, "Crucify him!" (Mark 15:14)
Luke 23:20 Wanting to release Jesus, Pilate appealed to them again.
    21 But they kept shouting, "Crucify him! Crucify him!"
    22 For the third time he spoke to them: "Why? What crime has this man committed? I have found in him no grounds for the death penalty. Therefore I will have him punished and then release him." (Luke 23:16)

Having failed to gain the support of the people, Pilate decided to appeal next to the accusers' sense of humanity. By having Jesus scourged he hoped to satisfy their thirst for blood and avoid having to crucify Jesus in order to appease them. The order was given to the soldiers and Jesus was taken within the fortress to be scourged.

The Scourging of Jesus

John 19:1 Then Pilate took Jesus and had him flogged.

Prelude to Glory

Scourging among the Romans was a more severe punishment than among the Jews. The scourge was made of cords or thongs of leather, and especially of ox-hide. There was one sort with which slaves were beaten, the use of which was particularly dreadful. It was knotted with bones or heavy, indented circles of bronze. Sometimes the thongs, two or three in number, terminated in hooks. This type of scourge was called a "scorpion." There was no legal limit to the number of blows, as among the Jews. The accused was bound to a low pillar so that his back would be more accessible to the strokes. Then he was beaten with merciless severity, often to the point of death.

The scourging would not have taken more than a few minutes, but in Jesus' case the soldiers decided to have some fun with him while they had him under their control.

> **Mark 15:16** The soldiers led Jesus away into the palace (that is, the Praetorium) and called together the whole company of soldiers. (Matt. 27:27)
> **Matt. 27:28** They stripped him and put a scarlet robe on him, (Mark 15:17)
> 29 And then wove a crown of thorns and set it on his head. They put a staff in his right hand and knelt in front of him and mocked him. "Hail, king of the Jews!" they said. (Mark 15:18; John 19:2)
> 30 They spit on him, and took the staff and struck him on the head again and again. (Mark 15:19; John 19:3)

When the soldiers had finished having their fun, Jesus was once again brought out to a place where the accusers in the passageway between the fortress and the temple could see him. Mob hysteria had taken over the multitude outside the fortress and Pilate realized that any further appeal there would be futile. He also appreciated the fact that it was the leaders, not the people, who wanted Jesus dead and that any appeal for leniency would have to be made to them. Pilate hoped the sight of Jesus beaten and bleeding would satisfy them and he would be able to release him. Thus he made his final appeal to the leaders' reason and sense of justice while the people waited outside.

Trial of a King

Pilate's Sixth Attempt to Save Jesus

John 19:4 Once more Pilate came out and said to the Jews, "Look, I am bringing him out to you to let you know that I find no basis for a charge against him."

5 When Jesus came out wearing the crown of thorns and the purple robe, Pilate said to them, "Here is the man!"

6 As soon as the chief priests and their officials saw him, they shouted, "Crucify! Crucify!" But Pilate answered, "You take him and crucify him. As for me, I find no basis for a charge against him."

7 The Jews insisted, "We have a law, and according to that law he must die, because he claimed to be the Son of God."

There is no reason to believe Pilate was a religious man or that he had any particular inclination toward mercy. Tradition does claim, however, that later his wife was converted to Christianity. Even so, this last assertion by the Jews caused him to return and question Jesus further. Perhaps superstition was causing the fear that seemed to be coming over Pilate. He desperately wanted to retain the favor of the Jewish leaders but there was something about this man Jesus that awakened feelings of fear within Pilate when he contemplated sentencing him to death.

John 19:8 When Pilate heard this, he was even more afraid,

9 and he went back inside the palace. "Where do you come from?" he asked Jesus, but Jesus gave him no answer.

Matt. 27:12 When he was accused by the chief priests and the elders, he gave no answer. (Mark. 15:3)

13 Then Pilate asked him, "Don't you hear how many things they are accusing you of?" (Mark 15:4)

14 But Jesus made no reply, not even to a single charge—to the great amazement of the governor. (Mark 15:5)

John 19:10 "Do you refuse to speak to me?" Pilate said. "Don't you realize I have power either to free you or to crucify you?"

> **11** Jesus answered, "You would have no power over me if it were not given to you from above. Therefore the one who handed me over to you is guilty of a greater sin."

This is one of the most profound statements in the entire Bible. Pilate represented the power and might of the greatest military empire ever established on the earth. Rome's legions literally ruled the world. No power existed that was able to withstand Rome. Yet, here stood a lowly carpenter, the son of peasants, quietly and emphatically claiming for himself a power greater than any which Pilate possessed. If there were any lingering doubts as to who was in control of the events taking place, this one statement should have forever removed them. Jesus had rendered Pilate's soldiers helpless in the Garden of Gethsemane. Now Pilate himself stood there honestly believing he held Jesus' fate in his hands. Jesus corrected his assumption although Pilate probably never understood the full ramifications of Jesus' statement.

Another aspect of Jesus' answer bears comment also. Whom did Jesus mean by "the one who handed me over"? There are two possibilities. The obvious one is Judas and certainly he would pay a dear price if he hadn't done so already. The second possibility isn't quite so obvious but may in fact be the more probable of the two. That would be Caiaphas, the high priest, the man with the most to lose should Jesus reestablish the kingdom of David and sit upon an earthly throne. Judas may have acted in spite and certainly repented of his action as soon as he saw the full consequence of his deed. There is no record, however, of Caiaphas' showing the slightest remorse for his role. The scriptures leave the question unanswered and so must we, but it is interesting to notice that there is more than one possibility.

Pilate's Final Attempt to Save Jesus

> **John 19:12** From then on, Pilate tried to set Jesus free, but the Jews kept shouting, "If you let this man go, you are no friend of Caesar. Anyone who claims to be a king opposes Caesar."

Trial of a King

With this statement the Jews located Pilate's Achilles' heel. There can be no doubt that Pilate sincerely believed Jesus innocent of the charges brought against him. Nevertheless, Pilate lacked the personal strength of character to stand by his convictions. His fear of displeasing Caesar was greater than his fear of God. As a result he was left without a choice in the matter. He acted to preserve his position and thus Jesus' fate was sealed. The Jews, with the help of the Roman empire, had seen to it that the will of God would be carried out in perfect harmony with the divine plan established long before the earth's creation (Acts 2:23).

The Sentencing of Jesus

John 19:13 When Pilate heard this, he brought Jesus out and sat down on the judge's seat at a place known as The Stone Pavement (which in Aramaic is Gabbatha).
14 It was the day of Preparation of Passover Week, about the sixth hour. "Here is your king," Pilate said to the Jews.
Matt. 27:19 While Pilate was sitting on the judge's seat, his wife sent him this message: "Don't have anything to do with that innocent man, for I have suffered a great deal today in a dream because of him."

This passage has lent itself to much speculation. There is no doubt that Pilate's wife was aware of the previous night's activities when Judas and the others arrived to obtain the escort of soldiers. It is entirely possible she and Pilate discussed the matter somewhat before going to bed. This may have caused Jesus to be on her mind when she went to sleep and, as is often the case, prompted her dream. It is also possible she had heard Jesus speaking in the temple and knew he was not guilty of the Jews' charges. As has been mentioned before, tradition supports the belief that she became a Christian. To any extent, dreams were considered to be omens and she desperately wanted her husband to refuse the Jewish leaders' request. Such, however, was not to be, for the crowd, still stirred up, continued to cry for blood.

John 19:15 But they shouted, "Take him away! Take him away! Crucify him!" "Shall I crucify your king?" Pilate asked. "We have no king but Caesar," the chief priests answered. (Luke 23:23)

Matt. 27:24 When Pilate saw that he was getting nowhere, but that instead an uproar was starting, he took water and washed his hands in front of the crowd. "I am innocent of this man's blood," he said. "It is your responsibility!"

25 All the people answered, "Let his blood be on us and on our children!"

If ever a people named their own poison, this statement was it. For two thousand years the Jewish nation has never known peace. It is impossible to study the history of the Jews through the ensuing years without realizing the significance that statement has had on their national existence. In 1948 the nation of Israel was reestablished by an act of the United Nations but there has not been a day since that their national existence has not been challenged. The Jewish people have suffered during the last two thousand years as no group of people has ever suffered.

Concerning the proper blame for Jesus' murder, A. T. Robertson in his *Harmony of the Gospels* made the following observation:

> Pilate, of course, could not escape full legal and moral responsibility for his cowardly surrender to the Sanhedrin to keep his office. The guilt of the Sanhedrin (both Pharisees and Sadducees united in the demand for the blood of Jesus) is beyond dispute. It is impossible to make a mere political issue out of it and to lay all the blame on the Sadducees, who feared a revolution. The Pharisees began the attacks against Jesus on theological and ecclesiastical grounds. The Sadducees later joined the conspiracy against Christ. Judas was a mere tool of the Sanhedrin, who had his resentments and grievances to avenge. There is guilt enough for all the plotters in the greatest wrong of the ages.

Luke 23:24 So Pilate decided to grant their demand.

25 He released the man who had been thrown into

Trial of a King

prison for insurrection and murder, the one they asked for, and surrendered Jesus to their will. (Matt. 27:26; Mark 15:15; John 19:16)

It is indeed ironic that the name of the man they released. Barabbas, means "Son of the Father," while the true Son of God was sent to the cross.

The Way of the Cross

The actual sentencing of Jesus probably took place around eight o'clock in the morning. The death warrant had to be prepared and signed by Pilate, and the plaque bearing the inscription had to be prepared.

When a prisoner was condemned to death under Roman law, certain rituals were performed to ensure that the death would serve as a deterrent to others. One such ritual was the parade of the accused through the city streets. Four soldiers would be assigned to each of the accused. In Jesus' case, that would mean a total of twelve soldiers plus a centurion who would be in command of the group. Additionally, a plaque would be prepared stating the crime for which the accused was being put to death. The plaque was carried ahead of the accused so everyone would know why he was being executed. In Jesus' case, Pilate himself determined what was to be written on the sign.

Some have contended that the Gospel reports of what the sign said contradict one another. This is simply not the case. In the first place, the sign was written in three languages—Greek, Latin, and Aramaic. The different writers could simply have reported different wording based on the particular language each chose to report. That, however, need not be used as an excuse for the different reports. There is an interesting little diagram that can be drawn to reconcile the reports nicely.

The Plaque's Inscription

Matthew: This is Jesus -- ------------, the King of the Jews
Mark: ----- -- ------ -- ------------, the King of the Jews

Prelude to Glory

Luke:	This is ------ -- ------------, the King of the Jews
John:	----- -- Jesus of Nazareth, the King of the Jews

Total   This is Jesus of Nazareth, the King of the Jews

John 19:19 Pilate had a notice prepared and fastened to the cross. It read: "Jesus of Nazareth, the King of the Jews."
    20 Many of the Jews read this sign, for the place where Jesus was crucified was near the city, and the sign was written in Aramaic, Latin and Greek.
    21 The chief priests of the Jews protested to Pilate, "Do not write 'The King of the Jews,' but that this man claimed to be king of the Jews."
    22 Pilate answered, "What I have written, I have written."

Pilate had acquiesced on every other point. He would not be moved on this one. The inscription stood as he had first directed. It is possible that Pilate believed the inscription but weakness of character prevented him from doing anything more. In any case, the small group left the fortress to weave its way slowly through the streets of Jerusalem. The route has come to be known as "the way of the cross."

Mark 15:20 And when they had mocked him, they took off the purple robe and put his own clothes on him. Then they led him out to crucify him. (Matt. 27:31)

The route from the fortress to the Damascus gate would have led through the newer part of Jerusalem. The fortress was in the northeast section and the gate in the north wall. It would not have been more than a quarter mile or so from the fortress to the gate. This was a suburban area and would not have had as many shops as would the southeastern section of the city. This may account for the fact that there seem to have been more women than men on the streets.

Trial of a King

At that time of morning there would actually be very few people up and about. The mental image of the streets' being lined with spectators is a common misconception. The city was preparing for a major holiday and very few were aware of the fact that Jesus had even been arrested, much less was being led out for crucifixion. The few on the streets who followed the procession grew as time passed and the wailing and lamenting mentioned is a mid-East custom even today. The sorrow was for the fact and not the person. To the average citizen these were just three more misfortunates who had fallen victim to the Roman oppression, an all too common sight in first-century Jerusalem.

John 19:16 Finally Pilate handed him over to them to be crucified. So the soldiers took charge of Jesus.
17 Carrying his own cross, he went out to The Place of the Skull (which in Aramaic is called Golgotha).

The "cross" Jesus carried was more than likely just the crossbeam and not the entire cross. This piece alone would have been very heavy, especially for a man who had just undergone a Roman scourging. As it happened, a man from Cyrene was just coming in from the country. He was in all probability a pilgrim coming in for the Passover.

Matt. 27:32a As they were going out, they met a man from Cyrene, named Simon . . .
Mark 15:21 . . . the father of Alexander and Rufus,
Matt. 27:32b . . . and they forced him to carry the cross.
Luke 23:27 A large number of people followed him, including women who mourned and wailed for him.
28 Jesus turned and said to them, "Daughters of Jerusalem, do not weep for me; weep for yourselves and for your children.
29 For the time will come when you will say, 'Blessed are the barren women, the wombs that never bore and the breasts that never nursed!'
30 Then 'they will say to the mountains, "Fall on us!" and to the hills, "Cover us!"'
31 For if men do these things when the tree is green, what will happen when it is dry?"

Prelude to Glory

Jesus' comments here are almost identical to those made in Matthew chapter twenty-four. Here, as well as there, he was talking about the destruction of Jerusalem which would come to pass some forty years later. It is virtually impossible for us in twentieth-century America to visualize the despicable conditions that prevailed in Jerusalem during the siege by the Romans in A.D. 70. The degradation of the Israelites can be shown by one short incident reported by Josephus.

> She then attempted a most unnatural thing; and snatching up her son, who was a child sucking at her breast, she said, "O thou miserable infant! For whom shall I preserve you in this war, this famine, and this sedition? As to the war with the Romans, if they preserve our lives, we must be slaves! This famine also will destroy us, even before that slavery comes upon us; yet are these seditious rogues more terrible than both the other. Come on, be thou my food, and be thou a fury to these seditious varlets and a byeword to the world, which is all that is now wanting to complete the calamities of us Jews." As soon as she had said this, she slew her son; and then roasted him, and ate the one half of him and kept the other half by her concealed. (Wars VI, IV, 4)

Summary

Such was the manner in which Caiaphas was able to manipulate both the people and the Roman governor into giving him the life of Jesus. Little did he realize that his ambition was serving the purpose of God and opening the kingdom of heaven to all mankind. This did not remove the guilt for his deeds but proved that God does indeed "work in mysterious ways" to accomplish his purposes.

* * * * *

Men of Israel, listen to this: Jesus of Nazareth was a man accredited by God to you by miracles, wonders and signs, which God did among you through him, as you yourselves know. This man was handed over to you by God's set purpose and foreknowledge; and you, with the help of wicked men, put him to death by nailing him to the cross.

Acts 2:22–23

CHAPTER SEVEN

Death at Golgotha

It was nine o'clock in the morning and Jerusalem was coming to life in anticipation of the most important day of the religious year. This was the day of the Passover, a day of remembrance and a day of expectation.

Every household and every person, especially the young, would be reminded that on this day some fifteen hundred years before God had freed their forefathers from the cruel bondage of slavery in which they had lived for four hundred years in the land of Egypt.

It was also a great day of expectation. It was commonly believed that on this day God would deliver to them the promised Messiah who, like Moses, would once again free them from their bondage and reestablish the glory of the ancient kingdom of Israel. Likewise, David's throne would be restored and the new king would rule the people with justice and wisdom just as Solomon had.

The Morning Sacrifice at the Temple

All seventeen thousand priests and Levites were on duty at the temple making the final preparations for the great celebration. The morning prayers had gotten underway and the first sacrifices of the day were being laid upon the altar. This offering was called the "whole" offering and consisted of a lamb killed before the altar and then cut into several parts, each part being given to a different priest.

Caiaphas, the high priest, would have made this offering on the day of the Passover. All would have been in readiness when he arrived to offer the sacrifice. The lesser officials who had charge of

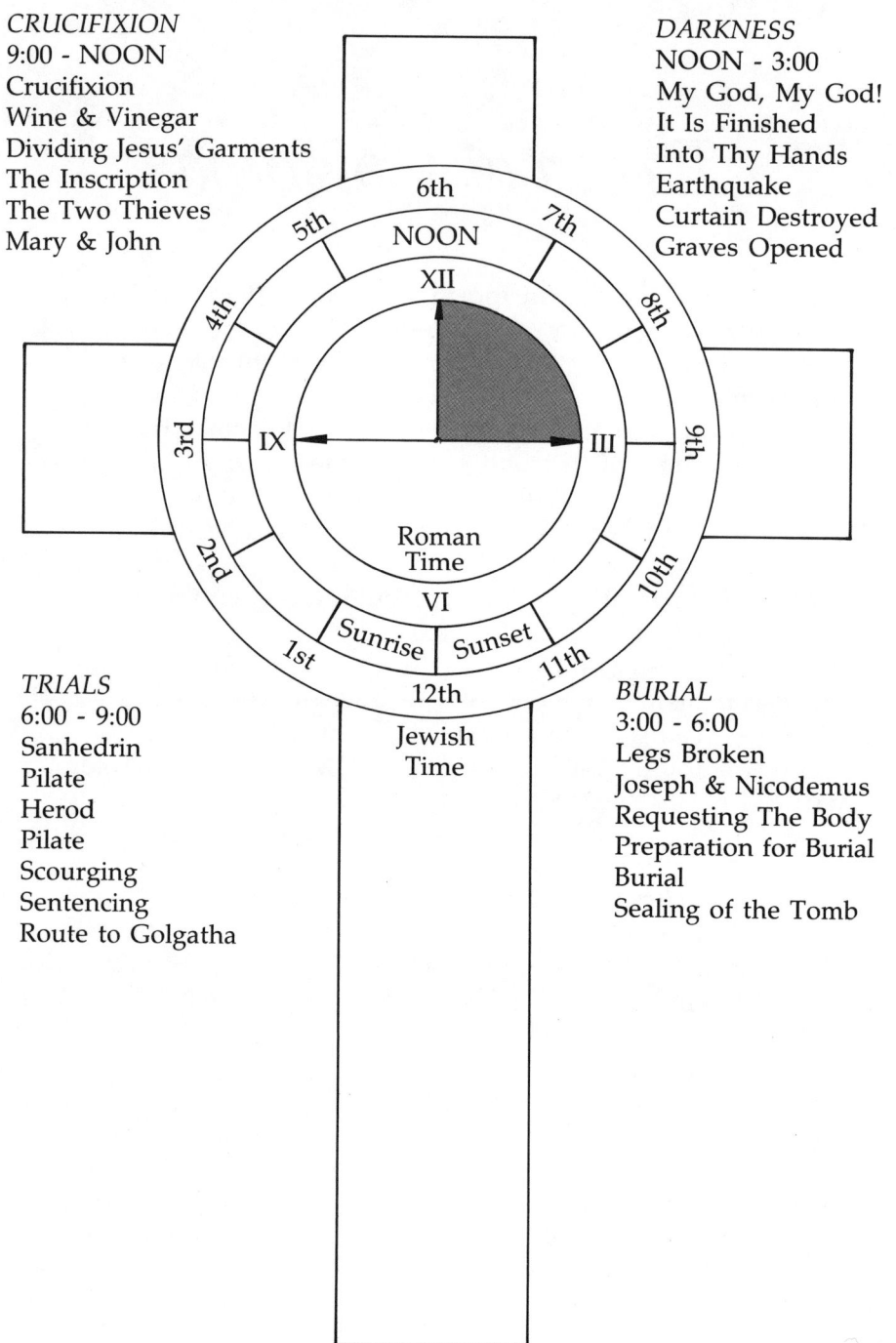

DAY OF CRUCIFIXION

CRUCIFIXION
9:00 - NOON
Crucifixion
Wine & Vinegar
Dividing Jesus' Garments
The Inscription
The Two Thieves
Mary & John

DARKNESS
NOON - 3:00
My God, My God!
It Is Finished
Into Thy Hands
Earthquake
Curtain Destroyed
Graves Opened

TRIALS
6:00 - 9:00
Sanhedrin
Pilate
Herod
Pilate
Scourging
Sentencing
Route to Golgatha

BURIAL
3:00 - 6:00
Legs Broken
Joseph & Nicodemus
Requesting The Body
Preparation for Burial
Burial
Sealing of the Tomb

Death at Golgotha

making the preparations would have slept at the temple the night before and risen at early dawn to complete the arrangements. Also, the cleansing ceremony for the high priest would have been completed and at precisely nine o'clock the high priest would have approached the altar.

The actual sacrifice is described in the Mishnah as follows:

> When the High Priest came in (to the Sanctuary) to prostrate himself, three (priests) held him, one by his right hand and one by his left hand, and one by the precious stones (Exod. 28:9ff.); and when the officer heard the sound of the High Priest's feet as he came out, he raised the curtain for him, and he went in and prostrated himself and came out. Then his brethren the priests went in and prostrated themselves and came out. . . .
>
> When the High Priest was minded to burn the offering, he used to ascend the Ramp having the Prefect at his right hand. When he had reached half way, the Prefect took him by the right hand and led him up. The first priest stretched out to him the head and the hind-leg, and he laid his hands on them and threw them [into the fire]. The second priest then gave the first one the two fore-legs and he gave them to the High Priest who laid his hands upon them and threw them. The second priest then slipped away and departed. In like manner they held out to him the rest of the members [of the offering] and he laid his hands on them. When he was so minded he only lay his hands on them while others threw them. Then he walked around the altar. Where did he begin? From the corner at the south-east, and so to the north-east and to the north-west and to the south-west. They gave him the wine for the drink-offering, and the Prefect stood by each horn of the altar with a towel in his hand, and two priests stood at the table of the fat pieces with two silver trumpets in their hands. They blew a prolonged, a quivering, and a prolonged blast. Then they came and stood by the priest with the cymbals, the one on his right and the other on his left. When the High Priest stooped to pour out the drink-offering the Prefect waved the towel, the priest with the cymbals clashed them and Levites broke forth into singing. When they reached a break in the singing they blew upon the trumpets and the people prostrated themselves; at every break there was a blowing of the trumpet and at every blowing of the trumpet a prostration. This was the rite of the Daily Whole-Offering in the service of the House of our God.

This was the singing which the Levites used to sing in the Temple. On the first day they sang . . ., on the fifth day they sang "Sing we merrily unto God our strength, make a cheerful noise unto the God of Jacob." (Mish. Tamid, 7.1–4)

A different song was sung by the Levites on each of the seven days of the week. Every Thursday the song was "Sing we merrily unto God" (Psalm 81). It is so ironic this particular psalm was sung on the day Jesus was crucified that it bears quoting at this point.

> Sing for joy to God our strength;
>   shout aloud to the God of Jacob!
> Begin the music, strike the tambourine,
>   play the melodious harp and lyre.
>
> Sound the ram's horn at the New Moon,
>   and when the moon is full, on the day of our Feast;
>   this is a decree for Israel,
>   an ordinance of the God of Jacob.
> He established it as a statute for Joseph
>   when he went out against Egypt,
>   where we heard a language we did not understand.
>
> He says, "I removed the burden from their shoulders;
>   their hands were set free from the basket.
> In your distress you called and I rescued you,
>   I answered you out of a thundercloud;
>   I tested you at the waters of Meribah.
>
> "Hear, O my people, and I will warn you—
>   if you would but listen to me, O Israel!
> You shall have no foreign god among you;
>   you shall not bow down to an alien god.
> I am the LORD your God,
>   who brought you up out of Egypt.
> Open wide your mouth and I will fill it.
>
> But my people would not listen to me;
>   Israel would not submit to me.
> So I gave them over to their stubborn hearts
>   to follow their own devices.
>
> "If my people would but listen to me,
>   if Israel would follow my ways,
>   how quickly would I subdue their enemies

Death at Golgotha

Golgotha

and turn my hand against their foes!
Those who hate the LORD would cringe before him,
   and their punishment would last forever.
But you would be fed with the finest of wheat;
   with honey from the rock I would satisfy you." (Ps. 81)

The Morning Sacrifice at Golgotha

Mark 15:22   They brought Jesus to the place called Golgotha (which means The Place of the Skull). (Matt. 27:33; Luke 23:33)

Skull Hill

There is no way to establish with certainty the exact location of Calvary or of the tomb in which Jesus was buried. There is strong tradition, however, that points to a place somewhere outside the north wall of the city. According to scripture Jesus was crucified "outside the city" (John 19:17, 20; Heb. 13:12) at a place called "the skull." *Calvary* in Latin and *Golgotha* in Hebrew both mean "skull." There is only one place around Jerusalem which has borne and still bears the name Skull Hill. It is just outside the north wall, near the old "Damascus Gate." It is a rocky ledge, some thirty feet high, just above "Jeremiah's Grotto," which bears a striking resemblance to a human skull. In front of Skull Hill is a large flat area that could well have served as an execution ground. The Romans usually had a specific site they used for executions. This area would have been near the Damascus highway which is also in accord with scripture (Matt. 27:39; Mark 15:29).

> **Matt. 27:34** There they offered him wine to drink, mixed with gall; but after tasting it, he refused to drink it. (Mark 15:23)

It was customary among the Romans to give the person to be crucified a stupefying potion of wine and myrrh. This, according to Mark, is what was offered to Jesus while Matthew refers to the myrrh as "gall." The potion was intended to stupefy the person and was considered a gesture of mercy. Jesus, however, did not choose to be rendered semiconscious. There were still things to be taken care of before his task was finished.

> **Luke 23:33** There they crucified him, along with the criminals—one on his right, the other on his left. (John 19:18)

A Roman Crucifixion

Crucifixion was not a Jewish mode of capital punishment. It was an ancient rite and is said to have been devised by the Semiramis. It was used by the Persians, Assyrians, Egyptians, Carthaginians, Scythians, Greeks, Romans, and ancient Germans. It was a most shameful and degrading punishment that the Romans used for robbers, assassins, and rebels. It was especially the punishment of criminal slaves.

There were several different types of crosses used for crucifixions but the description of the cross on which Jesus was crucified

Death at Golgotha

The Damascus Gate

ROMAN CROSS

Diagram—Roman Cross

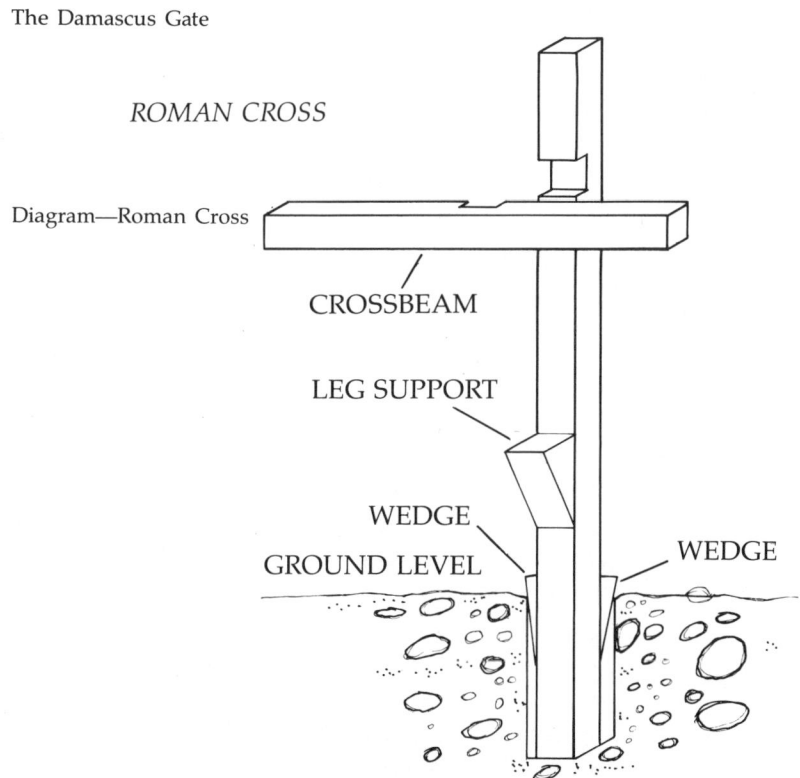

definitely identifies it as the type commonly depicted in paintings today in which the longer piece extends above the crossbar. As shown in the above drawing, there was a rest for the feet which enabled the victim to support the body with the legs. This was necessary if the punishment was intended to be prolonged without the victim's dying of suffocation. The ordinary representations of the cross in paintings are incorrect inasmuch as they make it appear larger and heavier than it really was. It was not usually more than ten feet high, so that when erect and planted in the earth, the feet of the victim were actually not far above the ground.

The condemned man was first stripped of his clothing, which seem to have been the prerequisite of the executioners. He was then fastened to the cross while it was lying on the ground. His arms were stretched out and tied to the crossbar between the elbow and the shoulder, and large spikes were driven through his hands and feet. Then the cross was lifted and thrust into the ground, and wedges were used to secure the cross in place.

The victim was left to hang in this position until death slowly came to his relief. This usually required two or three days, though some lingered even longer. A fact which is not usually stressed is that crucifixion proved fatal, not so much by loss of blood—since the wounds in the hands and feet did not lacerate any large blood vessels—as by the slow process of nervous irritation and exhaustion.

The Dividing of Jesus' Garments

John 19:23 When the soldiers crucified Jesus, they took his clothes, dividing them into four shares, one for each of them, with the undergarment remaining. This garment was seamless, woven in one piece from top to bottom.

24 "Let's not tear it," they said to one another. "Let's decide by lot who will get it." This happened that the scripture might be fulfilled which said, "They divided my garments among them and cast lots for my clothing." So this is what the soldiers did. (Matt. 27:35; Mark 15:24)

Death at Golgotha

Matt. 27:36 And sitting down, they kept watch over him there.
Mark 15:25 It was the third hour when they crucified him.
Luke 23:34 Jesus said, "Father, forgive them, for they do not know what they are doing."

Jesus' clothes had been removed before he was nailed to the cross, as was the custom. As booty for performing the execution the soldiers were given any possession which the victim had. In Jesus' case that would be limited to his clothing. The casting of lots was a method by which sticks were tossed in a dice-like fashion, and the position in which the sticks came to rest determined the winner. From his position on the cross Jesus was able to look down on the soldiers, and the sight no doubt gave rise to his prayer in their behalf.

The Inscription on the Cross

Luke 23:38 There was a written notice above him, which read: "This is the King of the Jews."
Matt. 27:38 Two robbers were crucified with him, one on his right and one on his left. (Mark 15:27)

The sign with the inscription that now was nailed to the cross above Jesus' head was the one that had been carried before him as he was led through the streets from the fortress of Antonia to Calvary. Each of the two thieves would have had a sign over his head as well.

The First Three Hours on the Cross

Matt. 27:39 Those who passed by hurled insults at him, shaking their heads
40 and saying, "You who are going to destroy the temple and build it in three days, save yourself! Come down from the cross, if you are the Son of God!" (Mark 15:29–30)
Luke 23:35 The people stood watching, and the rulers even

Prelude to Glory

	sneered at him. They said, "He saved others, let him save himself if he is the Christ of God; the Chosen One."
Matt. 27:41	In the same way the chief priests, the teachers of the law and the elders mocked him. (Mark 15:31)
42	"He saved others," they said, "but he can't save himself! He's the king of Israel! Let him come down now from the cross, and we will believe in him. (Mark 15:32)
43	He trusts in God. Let God rescue him now if he wants him, for he said, 'I am the Son of God.'"
Luke 23:36	The soldiers also came up and mocked him. They offered him wine vinegar
37	and said, "If you are the king of the Jews, save yourself."

The cross on which Jesus hung was not far from the road on which the travelers from Damascus came to celebrate the Passover. It was not uncommon in those days for Roman crosses to be seen along the main roads in Palestine. The time allowed for travel would end at noon when a blast of trumpets from the temple would announce the official beginning of the Passover period. These late arrivals would have been hurrying to get settled before the onset of the ceremonies. No doubt it was the title above his head which caused their derisive comments.

Some of the chief priests were at the cross which indicates they had probably been excused from their tasks at the temple to be sure the people stayed sufficiently riled up to keep Jesus on the cross until he was dead. Normally these priests would have been involved in the ceremonies at the temple. Some of the scribes and elders were also present. This was probably the delegation from the Sanhedrin that had escorted Jesus to Pilate.

The last to be named were the soldiers. As this type of gruesome affair was all too commonplace for these men, they seem to have enjoyed breaking the monotony by devising new ways to torment their prisoners. The wine vinegar mentioned here was wine that had soured. This would have been offered in place of water as a further source of entertainment and torture.

Death at Golgotha

The Two Thieves

Matt. 27:44 In the same way the robbers who were crucified with him also heaped insults on him.

Luke 23:39 One of the criminals who hung there hurled insults at him: "Aren't you the Christ? Save yourself and us!"

40 But the other criminal rebuked him. "Don't you fear God," he said, "since you are under the same sentence?

41 We are punished justly, for we are getting what our deeds deserve. But this man has done nothing wrong."

42 Then he said, "Jesus, remember me when you come into your kingdom."

43 Jesus answered him, "I tell you the truth, today you will be with me in paradise."

This short episode is recorded only by Luke, using just five verses to relay the entire conversation. Yet, this exchange has inspired hundreds if not thousands of sermons about Jesus' fellow prisoners, who have become known as the "good and the bad thief."

Again we see a form of the belief which Pilate had manifested earlier. While Pilate lacked the courage to carry through with his basic inclination about Jesus, the thief had no such inhibitions. Pilate had much to lose and, in his own mind, not enough to gain to warrant siding with Jesus. The thief, on the other hand, had nothing to lose and everything to gain. What caused his belief in the man who hung on the cross next to his? Was it possibly the eyes again? Did he see something in Jesus' eyes that melted his heart, or had he had some previous encounter with Jesus and his teachings that brought forth this eleventh-hour confession?

Whatever the motivation, there is an extremely important point here that should not be overlooked. Jesus stated emphatically that the thief would be with him in paradise that very day. This negates much erroneous teaching in the religious world today concerning the soul of man following its separation from the body. Jesus makes it clear that disembodied spirits immediately enter the spiritual realm. This same fact is illustrated in the parable of Lazarus and the rich man (Luke 16:19–31).

Woman, Behold Thy Son

John 19:25 Near the cross of Jesus stood his mother, his mother's sister, Mary the wife of Clopas, and Mary Magdala.
   26 When Jesus saw his mother there, and the disciple whom he loved standing nearby, he said to his mother, "Dear woman, here is your son,"
   27 and to the disciple, "Here is your mother." From that time on, this disciple took her into his home.

John had evidently left Jesus following the sentencing by Pilate and gone to get Mary. He omits anything which happened between the sentencing in Antonia and the dividing of Jesus' garments. Many commentators feel this is because John was not present during this period. John arrived at Golgotha with Mary and perhaps the other women, also. As he stood there with them, Jesus saw him and assigned the care of Mary to John, and "from that time on" Mary became a part of John's household. The wording here has caused some to believe that John actually owned a home in Jerusalem. This possibility is discussed in the next chapter and has a bearing on understanding the various Gospel reports of the visits to the tomb.

The Sixth Hour

The sixth hour, or noon, marked the official beginning of the Passover period. Once begun, the celebration would last until the appearance of the first three stars of evening following the sunset that ended the twenty-first of Nisan. The Jewish leaders had developed a curious method for telling the people when the Passover period had begun.

> Early on the forenoon of the fourteenth of Nisan the feast of the Passover may be said to have begun. In Galilee, no work was done

all that day; in Judea it was continued till mid-day; the rule however, being that no new work was to be commenced, though that which was in hand might be carried on. The only exception to this was in the case of tailors, barbers, and those engaged in laundry. Even earlier than mid-day of the fourteenth it was no longer lawful to eat leaven. The strictest opinion fixes ten o'clock as the latest hour when leaven might be eaten, the more lax eleven. From that hour to twelve o'clock it was required to abstain from leaven, while at twelve any remaining leaven was to be solemnly destroyed, either by burning, immersing it in water, or scattering it to the winds. To secure strict obedience and uniformity, the exact time for destroying the leaven was thus made known: They laid two desecrated cakes of a thanks-offering on a bench in the porch of the temple. So long as they lay there, all the people might eat leavened bread; when one of them was removed, they abstained from eating, but they did not burn it; when both were removed, all the people burnt the leaven. (Mish., Pes. 10.5)

On this particular day just as the priest removed the second cake from the bench the sky began to grow dark and within minutes darkness prevailed throughout the whole land.

Mark 15:33 At the sixth hour darkness came over the whole land until the ninth hour.

There is no explanation known to science that could account for this phenomenon. Some have suggested an eclipse of the sun but anyone who has ever witnessed an eclipse knows it just lasts for a few minutes. This darkness lasted for three hours and evidently ended as suddenly as it had begun.

Many applications have been made of this darkness within the theology of Christendom. Some believe it caused by God's removing his presence or turning his back on the scene at Calvary. Some have even suggested that for three hours inanimate nature hid her face in shame at the "unspeakable wickedness of men." Others suggest God may have meant the darkness to be creation's symbolic mourning for Jesus. It was God who had said, "Let there be light;" it was certainly within his prerogative to eliminate it.

Any application of the darkness at Calvary I leave to the pen of the theologian. That being as it may, Jesus' physical suffering during the next three hours would certainly have been lessened without the scorching heat of the noonday sun beating down upon his naked body. This alone would have been sufficient justification for the darkness.

The Second Three Hours on the Cross

Mark 15:34   And at the ninth hour Jesus cried out in a loud voice. *"Eloi, Eloi, lama sabachthani?"*—which means, "My God, My God, why have you forsaken me?" (Matt. 27:46)

The scriptures are silent as to anything that transpired at Calvary between noon and three o'clock in the afternoon. At three o'clock, however, Jesus cried out, "My God, My God, why have you forsaken me?" These words, spoken from the cross in the midst of the darkness, are the opening words of Psalm 22. Although this psalm was written more than a thousand years before Jesus was crucified, it described his very thoughts while on the cross. For this reason, Psalm 22 is inserted here in its entirety.

My God, my God, why have you forsaken me?
Why are you so far from saving me, so far from the words of my groaning?
O my God, I cry out by day, but you do not answer,
   by night, and am not silent.

Yet you are enthroned as the Holy One;
   you are the praise of Israel.
In you our fathers put their trust;
   they trusted and you delivered them.
They cried to you and were saved;
   in you they trusted and were not disappointed.

But I am a worm and not a man,
   scorned by men and despised by the people.
All who see me mock me;
   they hurl insults, shaking their heads:
"He trusts in the LORD;
   let the Lord rescue him.
Let him deliver him, since he delights in him."

Death at Golgotha

Yet you brought me out of the womb;
  you made me trust in you even at my mother's breast.
From birth I was cast upon you;
  from my mother's womb you have been my God.
Do not be far from me,
  for trouble is near and there is no one to help.

Many bulls surround me;
  strong bulls of Bashan encircle me.
Roaring lions tearing their prey
  open their mouths wide against me.
I am poured out like water,
  and all my bones are out of joint.
My heart has turned to wax;
  it has melted away within me.
My strength is dried up like a potsherd,
  and my tongue sticks to the roof of my mouth;
  you lay me in the dust of death.
Dogs have surrounded me;
  a band of evil men has encircled me,
  they have pierced my hands and my feet.
I can count all my bones;
  people stare and gloat over me.

They divide my garments among them
  and cast lots for my clothing.

But you, O Lord, be not far off;
  O my Strength, come quickly to help me.
Deliver my life from the sword,
  my precious life from the power of the dogs.
Rescue me from the mouth of the lions;
  save my from the horns of the wild oxen.

I will declare your name to my brothers;
  in the congregation I will praise you.
You who fear the Lord, praise him!
  All you descendants of Jacob, honor him!
  Revere him, all you descendants of Israel!
For he has not despised or disdained the
  suffering of the afflicted one;
he has not hidden his face from him
  but has listened to his cry for help.

Prelude to Glory

From you comes my praise in the great assembly;
   before those who fear you will I fulfill my vows.
The poor will eat and be satisfied;
   they who seek the LORD will praise him—
   may your hearts live forever!
All the end of the earth will remember and turn to the LORD,
   and all the families of the nations
   will bow down before him,
for dominion belongs to the LORD
   and he rules over the nations.

All the rich of the earth will feast and worship;
   all who go down to the dust will kneel before him—
   those who cannot keep themselves alive.
Posterity will serve him;
   future generations will be told about the LORD.
They will proclaim his righteousness to a people yet unborn—
   for he has done it. (Ps. 22)

Sacrificing the Passover Lamb

The sacrifice of the Passover lambs began at three o'clock in the afternoon. Normally the evening sacrifice was slain at two-thirty and offered at three-thirty. On the fourteenth of Nisan, however, it was moved forward one hour so that by three o'clock the slaying of the Passover lambs could begin.

The first of the three divisions of Israelites was admitted with their Passover lambs into the Court of the Priests. Each division must consist of not less than thirty persons (3 × 10, the symbolical number of the Divine and of completeness). Immediately the massive gates were closed behind them. The priests drew a threefold blast from their silver trumpets when the Passover lamb was slain. Altogether the scene was most impressive. All along the court up to the altar of burnt offering, priests stood in two rows, one holding golden, the other silver, bowls. In these the blood of the Passover lambs, which each Israelite slew for himself (as representative of his company at the Passover Supper), was caught up by a priest, who handed it to his colleague, receiving back an empty bowl; and so the bowls with the blood were passed up to the priest at the altar, who threw it

Death at Golgotha

against the base of the altar. While this was going on, a most solemn hymn of praise was sung, the Levites leading the song, and the offerers either repeating after them or merely responding.

The sacrifices were then hung up on hooks along the court, or laid on staves which rested on the shoulders of two men, then flayed; the entrails taken out and cleaned; and the inside fat separated, put in a dish, salted, and placed on the fire of the altar of burnt offering. This completed the sacrifice.

When the first division of offerers was dismissed, the second division entered, and finally the third. The service was identical for each of the three divisions. Then the whole service was concluded by burning the incense and trimming the lamps for the night.

Sacrificing the Lamb of God

The land had been in darkness for almost three hours when Jesus cried out the words "Eloi, Eloi," which some misunderstood to be "Elijah, Elijah." It was just before three o'clock when this happened.

Matt. 27:47 When some of those standing there heard this, they said, "He's calling Elijah." (Mark 15:35)

John 19:28 Later, knowing that all was now completed, and so that the Scripture would be fulfilled, Jesus said, "I am thirsty."

29 A jar of wine vinegar was there, so they soaked a sponge in it, put the sponge on a stalk of the hyssop plant, and lifted it to Jesus' lips. (Matt. 27:48)

Matt. 27:49 But the rest said, "Leave him alone. Let's see if Elijah comes to save him." (Mark 15:36)

John 19:30 When he had received the drink, Jesus said, "It is finished."

Luke 23:46 Jesus called out with a loud voice, "Father, into your hands I commit my spirit." When he had said this, he breathed his last. (Matt. 27:50; Mark 15:37)

Prelude to Glory
The Fury of God

Only a parent could begin to understand the restraint required on God's part to allow the final scene at Calvary to be completed. When Jesus died, however, God's fury was no longer contained and the earth shook with great violence.

At the temple it had been an unusual afternoon. The sun had gone dark at noon and then, just as the knives were put to the Passover lambs, the temple and the ground beneath it began to quake.

> **Matt. 27:51** At that moment the curtain of the temple was torn in two from top to bottom. The earth shook and the rocks split. (Mark 15:38; Luke 23:45)

This was the sixty-foot curtain hanging floor to ceiling between the Holy Place and the Most Holy Place. Prior to this the Holy of Holies was accessible only by the high priest of the Jewish nation. This destroying of the curtain is commonly believed to indicate that Jesus' death opened the "dwelling place of God" to all mankind.

> **Matt. 27:52** The tombs broke open and the bodies of many holy people who had died were raised to life.
> **53** They came out of the tombs, and after Jesus' resurrection they went into the holy city and appeared to many people.

It is extremely difficult to imagine what the effect of these phenomena must have had on the people witnessing them. The day had begun as one of national celebration and culminated days of preparation. The population of the city had more than doubled with the arrival of the many pilgrims who had come to celebrate the Passover. Those at the temple were not aware of the fact that this earthquake coincided exactly with the time of Jesus' death or that Jesus had died at the exact time prescribed for the sacrifice of the Passover lambs. They had no way, therefore, of making any connection between the two events. The citizens of Jerusalem surely assumed it was simply an earthquake occurring in the

Death at Golgotha

normal fashion. Those at the cross, however, and one man in particular, the Roman centurion, appear to have put it all together.

Matt. 27:54 When the centurion and those with him who were guarding Jesus saw the earthquake and all that had happened, they were terrified, and exclaimed, "Surely he was the Son of God!" (Mark 15:39; Luke 23:47)

Mark 15:40 Some women were there watching from a distance. Among them were Mary Magdalene, Mary the mother of James the younger and of Joses, and Salome. (Matt. 27:56)

41 In Galilee these women had followed him and cared for his needs. Many other women who had come up with him to Jerusalem were also there. (Matt. 27:55; Luke 23:49)

Luke 23:48 When all the people who had gathered to witness this sight saw what took place, they beat their breasts and went away.

The earthquake ended and the darkness lifted. The two thieves hung in the afternoon sun. The body of Jesus still hung on the cross between them but not in pain and agony—Jesus was no longer in it.

* * * * *

And they sang a new song:

"You are worthy to take the scroll and to open its seals,
  because you were slain,
  and with your blood you purchased men for God
  from every tribe and language and people and nation.
You have made them to be a kingdom
  and priests to serve our God,
  and they will reign on the earth."

Revelation 5:9–10

CHAPTER EIGHT

The Garden Tomb

There is little doubt that Jesus died at approximately three o'clock in the afternoon on the fourteenth of Nisan. There is considerable controversy, however, as to what day of the week that was. The scriptures make it clear that Jesus died the day before a Sabbath. This has long been considered to be the seventh-day Sabbath; consequently the day of his death has been thought to be a Friday. The Catholic church accepted this position and instituted the celebration of Good Friday as a commemoration of the death. It has been shown (see Appendix C) that the fifteenth of Nisan was always a Sabbath and therefore the day following his death would have been a Sabbath irrespective of the day of the week on which it fell. This being the case, it becomes necessary to study other evidence which has a bearing on the day of his death if the day of the week is to be correctly identified.

My opinion is that there is not enough evidence to establish with absolute certainty any particular day of Christ's death. The vast weight of evidence, however, favors a Thursday crucifixion. For this reason a Thursday crucifixion is used in this work and is included in the timetable (Appendix B). Appendix C is an in-depth study of the evidence supporting both a Thursday and a Friday crucifixion.

Breaking The Prisoner's Legs

John 19:31 Now it was the day of Preparation, and the next day was to be a special Sabbath. Because the Jews did not want the bodies left on the crosses during the Sabbath, they asked Pilate to have the legs broken and the bodies taken down.

The Garden Tomb

The Garden Tomb

Prelude to Glory

The purpose of public crucifixions as carried out by the Roman government was both to punish offenders and to dissuade others from breaking the laws of Rome. This was accomplished by making the death slow and humiliating, and the victim might spend several days on a cross before death freed him. When it was necessary to speed up the death for any reason, the prisoner's legs would be broken by striking them at the knees with a large wooden club. This prevented the victim from supporting his body with his legs which in turn made it very difficult to breath. He could not hang by the arms in this position very long before the lungs would cease to function. Death would then be caused by suffocation.

> **John 19:32** The soldiers therefore came and broke the legs of the first man who had been crucified with Jesus, and then those of the other.
> **33** But when they came to Jesus and found that he was already dead, they did not break his legs.
> **34** Instead, one of the soldiers pierced Jesus' side with a spear, bringing a sudden flow of blood and water.

Jesus was already dead when the soldiers came to break his legs. This is further confirmed by the fact that blood and water both flowed from his side when he was pierced with the spear. The separation of the water from the blood is an undeniable medical confirmation of death. This separation only takes place at death and is evident in just a few minutes after the death takes place. Thus, there can be absolutely no doubt Jesus was dead before he was removed from the cross. Nothing short of death is known to modern medical science which can provide this phenomenon.

The question arises, if this is the case, what was the medical cause of the death of Jesus? There has been much speculation concerning the cause of Jesus' death but the main piece of evidence has been entirely overlooked. Jesus said:

> The reason my Father loves me is that I lay down my life—only to take it up again. No one takes it from me, but I lay it down of my own accord. I have authority to lay it down and authority to take it up again. (John 10:17–18)

The Garden Tomb

Here Jesus clearly stated that his life could not be taken from him but that he had the ability to leave the body and to return to it as he chose. Death had no power over him. If it had been necessary to wait for death to overtake Jesus, he would still be hanging on the cross. The reason there is no apparent medical reason for his death is that he did not die of medical causes. He departed the body at the time of his choosing just as he had said he would. He could have done this at any time he chose, whether on a cross or not.

John 19:35 The man who saw it has given testimony, and his testimony is true. He knows that he tells the truth, and he testifies so that you also may believe.

John here affirmed that he was an eye witness to Jesus' death on the cross and thus could testify to the truthfulness of the crucifixion account.

John 19:36 These things happened so that the scripture would be fulfilled: "Not one of his bones will be broken,"
  37 and, as another scripture says, "They will look on the one they have pierced."

Requesting the Body

The bodies of executed criminals were considered property of the Roman government. Usually, however, the body would be released to the next of kin for burial. Otherwise it would be buried by the state in a pauper's grave. In the case of Jesus, a man by the name of Joseph of Arimathea went to Pilate and requested the body.

Joseph of Arimathea

Arimathea is believed to be the same city as Ramah in Ephraim, where Samuel lived, ten miles northeast of Lydda. Joseph of Arimathea was a wealthy merchant in the city of Jerusalem. He

Prelude to Glory

was a member of the Sanhedrin (Mark 15:43) and a disciple of Jesus (John 19:38), but secretly "for fear of the Jews." It is ironic that this man who kept his association with Jesus a secret because of fear would be the one who now came forward to ask Pilate for the body while the apostles were all in hiding.

Joseph owned a garden outside the walls of the city where he had recently had his own tomb hewn out of rock. We are told by John that the garden was not far from the place where Jesus was crucified.

> **Mark 15:42** It was Preparation Day (that is, the day before the Sabbath). So as evening approached,
> **43** Joseph of Arimathea, a prominent member of the Council, who was himself waiting for the kingdom of God . . ., (Matt. 27:57)
> **John 19:38** . . . a disciple of Jesus, but secretly because he feared the Jews . . .
> **Luke 23:50** . . . a good and upright man,
> **51** . . . who had not consented to their decision and action.
> **Mark 15:43** . . . went boldly to Pilate and asked for Jesus' body. (Matt. 27:58; Luke 23:52)
> **44** Pilate was surprised to hear that he was already dead. Summoning the centurion, he asked him if Jesus had already died.
> **45** When he learned from the centurion that it was so, he gave the body to Joseph.

Joseph is identified here as a member of the Sanhedrin which tried Jesus that morning, but Luke specifically states he did not consent to their decision. Luke 22:71 indicates there was no disagreement over the sentence among those who were present that morning, therefore we know Joseph was not included among those whom Caiaphas chose to hear Jesus' case. This further supports the biased nature of those who voted to send Jesus to the cross.

Pilate was surprised to learn Jesus was already dead. He had given permission for his legs to be broken and he assumed Jesus was still alive at that time. He knew that death did not come fast on

The Garden Tomb

a cross even after the legs had been broken. He did not know nor could he have comprehended the fact that Jesus could lay down his life and take it up again at will. Therefore, he called the centurion who had been at the cross to confirm that Jesus was really dead in so short a time. Having thus satisfied himself he granted the body to Joseph.

If the centurion had left the cross immediately after it was discovered Jesus was dead, it would still have been close to four o'clock before Joseph could make his request of Pilate. Add some time for Pilate to ascertain that Jesus was dead and then for Joseph to return to Golgotha, and it must have been close to four-thirty when the body was removed from the cross. Joseph personally removed Jesus' body. He was joined by another of Jesus' secret disciples.

Nicodemus

Like Joseph of Arimathea, Nicodemus was a member of the upper class and of the Sanhedrin. Also like Joseph, he had been excluded from the morning trial. Nicodemus had once come to Jesus by night early in his ministry. It was Nicodemus who, when told that he must be born again, asked, "Can a man return to his mother's womb?" (John 3:4). He was a Pharisee who had defended Jesus before other Pharisees (John 7:50–51). Now he joined Joseph in preparing the body for burial.

> **John 19:39** He was accompanied by Nicodemus, the man who earlier had visited Jesus at night. Nicodemus brought a mixture of myrrh and aloes, about seventy-five pounds.

The two spices Nicodemus brought to prepare Jesus' body for the tomb are recognizable to us from earlier mentions in scripture. Myrrh, known in Hebrew as *mor*, was a fragrant substance derived from the liquids of various plants and trees. In Exodus 30:23 it was one of the ingredients of the "oil of holy ointment." It was used in Esther 2:12 in the beauty treatments of the kings' women and in Proverbs 7:17 as a perfume. Myrrh is one of the gifts which the wise men brought to the infant Jesus (Matt.

2:11). Mark 15:23 says it was mixed with wine and offered to Jesus on the cross.

Aloe is the name of a costly and sweet-smelling substance used for perfume. It is mentioned in Psalm 45:8; Proverbs 7:17; and Song of Solomon 4:14. The tree from which aloes was extracted was probably either the eaglewood or the white sandalwood.

These two spices were very expensive and only used by the very rich. Here they were used appropriately in the burial of King Jesus.

Preparation for Burial

The Egyptians had invented embalming hundreds of years before the time of Jesus but the process took weeks to complete. Joseph and Nicodemus had slightly more than an hour.

Even the method the Jews normally used to prepare a body for burial took more time than was available at the moment. Normally the body would have been taken to a place where it could be completely bathed. Once bathed it would have been entirely coated with a salve prepared by cooking a number of spices and blending them together. The resulting salve would then be rubbed over the entire body. The body would then be wrapped mummy-style in bandages with other spices sprinkled in the folds. Finally, the body would be placed in the burial shroud.

A Jewish burial shroud was roughly fourteen feet by three feet. The body would be laid on one end of the shroud, then the other end would be folded over it. The shroud would then be sewn along the three open edges. A napkin was tied around the head to keep the jaw closed and sometimes coins were placed on the eyes to keep the eyelids shut.

In Jesus' case it appears the disciples made only temporary provisions to preserve the body until after the Sabbath period had passed. The bathing and coating with salve would have

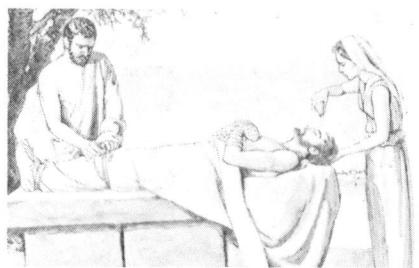

Jewish Burial Preparation

to wait until there was sufficient time. For the moment they merely removed the body from the cross, wrapped it in bandages, and placed it inside the shroud along with some seventy-five pounds of spices.

John 19:40   Taking Jesus' body, the two of them wrapped it with the spices, in strips of linen. This was in accordance with Jewish burial customs. (Matt. 27:59; Mark 15:46; Luke 23:53)

The Burial

John 19:41   At the place where Jesus was crucified, there was a garden, and in the garden a new tomb, in which no one had ever been laid.
       42   Because it was the Jewish day of Preparation and since the tomb was nearby, they laid Jesus there. (Matt. 27:60; Luke 23:54).
Matt. 27:60   He [Joseph] rolled a big stone in front of the entrance to the tomb and went away.

The Garden Tomb

Today there are two locations which compete for the honor of being recognized as the actual site of Jesus' tomb. One is the traditional site which is marked by the Church of the Holy Sepulchre and dates its claim back to the third century. This site is owned by the Catholic church. The other site is known as the Garden Tomb and has only been considered for the honor since late in the nineteenth century. In his book, *The Search for the Tomb of Jesus*, William McBirnie presents an exhaustive discussion of the strengths and weaknesses of the claims for each site.

My opinion is that the evidence against the tomb marked by the Church of the Holy Sepulchre is stronger than the evidence for the Garden Tomb. The actual site can never be more than speculation, but the Garden Tomb does provide us with an excellent example of the type of tomb in which Jesus was buried.

There were basically two types of tombs in use by the Jews during the first century, the communal or poor man's tomb and the rich man's tomb.

FIRST CENTURY COMMUNAL BURIAL CHAMBER

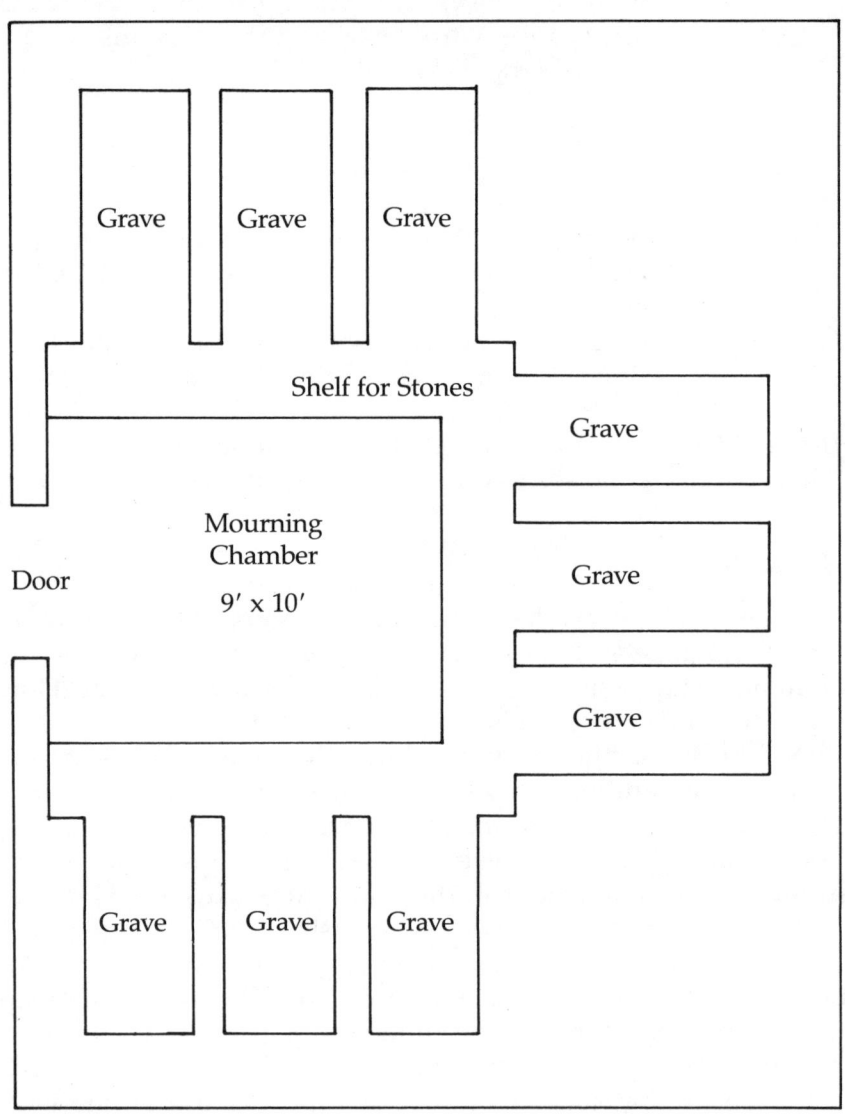

Diagram—First Century Communal Burial Chamber

The Garden Tomb

The Poor Man's Tomb

The communal or poor man's tomb was designed to accommodate nine to twelve bodies. From the outside one would enter first into the "mourning chamber" which was approximately ten feet square. The mourning chamber was designed to accommodate a small group of mourners. The Jews believed the grief of death could be overcome sooner if a person engaged in "exhaustive mourning." This was the purpose of the mourning chamber.

Around the walls of the chamber, about three feet from the ground, were the openings of tunnels approximately seven feet deep. These tunnels were generally two feet wide and two feet high. A body would be prepared for burial, then placed into one of the tunnels head first. The tunnel would then be sealed off with either stones and mortar or a single large stone.

This was definitely not the type of tomb into which Jesus was placed. There would be no way two angels could appear, one sitting at the head and the other at the feet of where Jesus lay (John 20:12). Also, this type of tomb would not have the large stone at the entrance as did Jesus' tomb (Mark 16:3–4).

The Rich Man's Tomb

The Garden Tomb is an outstanding example of a rich man's tomb, which was designed to accommodate only two bodies. The entrance led into the mourning chamber just as in a poor man's tomb. The burial chamber, however, was a completely separate room. Here the graves ran along the wall and resembled large bathtubs. The deceased would be laid in one of the two graves. A corpse in one of these tombs would be totally visible to those standing in the burial chamber until a large flat stone was laid on top of the grave and fitted into a notch which ran along the top of the grave to receive the stone. This arrangement lends itself perfectly to the description of the position of the angels in John 20:12.

Additionally, this type of tomb was sealed with a large stone which resembled a mill stone. A groove was cut in the rock along the outside of the tomb entrance in which the stone could roll. The groove sloped toward the door which made it easy for the

FIRST CENTURY RICH MAN'S TOMB

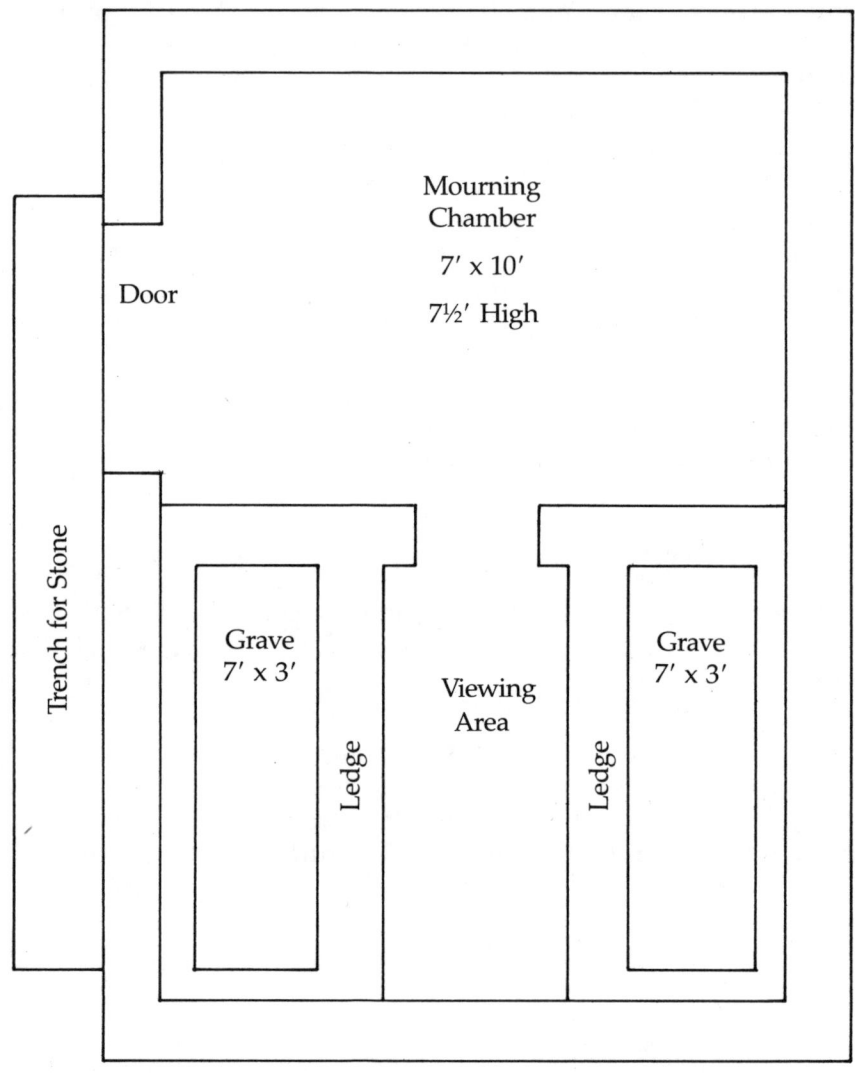

Diagram—Interior of Garden Tomb

The Garden Tomb

stone to be rolled across the door. It was considerably more difficult to roll the stone away from the door because that would be uphill. When the door was open a wedge placed under the stone would keep it from rolling back across the door. This is unmistakably the type of tomb into which Jesus' body was placed by Nicodemus and Joseph of Arimathea.

The Garden

We are told the tomb was in a garden. Inasmuch as the tomb had been dug for Joseph of Arimathea it is evident the garden belonged to him also. This would have been a garden very similar to the Garden of Gethsemane. It could have been as large as a couple of acres with paths winding among the trees. The tomb was probably in a secluded place near the back of the garden where there would have been some sort of cliff into which the tomb had been dug. It is also very possible there was more than one entrance to the garden. This would have been the type of peaceful setting in which the body of Jesus was laid to rest.

Jesus was placed in the tomb just prior to the sundown which began the most important of the Jewish national holidays. As his body was being laid to rest the Jewish nation was preparing to celebrate the Passover. The lambs had been killed and at that moment thousands were being cooked in the prescribed manner. This was the day of the preparation of the Passover (John 19:14), the day on which the lamb was killed.

It is the height of irony and the epitome of poetic justice that the Jews would kill Jesus on the Passover. The Passover had become the festival of anticipating the second redemption as well as celebrating the first. In every part of the world, especially in Palestine, Jewish celebrants looked to Passover eve with the hope that this night they would be freed from the bondage of Rome, just as their ancestors had been released from Egyptian slavery.

The Women

Mark 15:47 Mary Magdalene and Mary the mother of Joses saw where he was laid. (Matt. 27:61)
Luke 23:55 The women who had come with Jesus from

Prelude to Glory

Galilee followed Joseph and saw the tomb and how his body was laid in it.

The women who were at the cross witnessed the fact that Jesus' body was placed in the tomb. No less than five women were named and probably there were others. These women along with Joseph and Nicodemus provided ample testimony that the body was placed in a grave and that the grave was shut.

Luke 23:56 Then they went home and prepared spices and perfumes. But they rested on the Sabbath in obedience to the commandment.

There would not have been time before the onset of the Sabbath for the women to complete the cooking of the spices. No cooking was allowed on the seventh-day Sabbath and only that which was required for the feast was allowed on the Passover Sabbath. The spices would have had to wait until after the seventh-day Sabbath had ended on Saturday night.

Sealing the Tomb

Matt. 27:62 The next day, the one after Preparation Day, the chief priests and the Pharisees went to Pilate.
63 "Sir," they said, "we remember that while he was still alive that deceiver said, 'After three days I will rise again.'
64 So give the order for the tomb to be made secure until the third day. Otherwise, his disciples may come and steal the body and tell the people that he has been raised from the dead. This last deception will be worse than the first."

The Jews misquoted Jesus by claiming he had said "after" three days he would rise again. Even so, it is interesting to note that it was *through* the third day that they wanted the tomb to be made secure.

This request would have been made of Pilate just as the

The Garden Tomb

Passover Sabbath began. The "next day" began at sunset. The Jewish leaders, worried that Jesus' supporters would steal his body "during the night," would not have waited until morning to ask that the tomb be sealed.

The sealing would have been accomplished by placing a large piece of clay at the joint of the stone and the wall. An official insignia of some type would have been pressed into the soft clay leaving an imprint which could not be duplicated. The clay would then have hardened, providing a seal that would be broken if the stone were moved.

Sealing the tomb would serve a three fold purpose. First, there would be evidence if anyone moved the stone. This would prevent someone from removing the body and then claiming he had been raised. Second, it would provide a guard of Roman soldiers to ensure no one could tamper with the tomb. Third, because it was a criminal offense to break a Roman seal, it would serve as an effective deterrent to anyone inclined to steal the body. Getting caught in the attempt would mean time in prison if not worse.

Matt. 27:65 "Take a guard," Pilate answered. "Go, make the tomb as secure as you know how."
66 So they went and made the tomb secure by putting a seal on the stone and posting the guard.

The Roman soldiers would be held responsible if anything happened to the body they were assigned to guard. Since the seal was a guarantee that the contents were still within, we can be certain that before accepting this responsibility the soldiers opened the tomb and made sure the body was there. Only after personally viewing the body would they have sealed the tomb. This is absolute proof that Jesus' body was in the tomb when the seal was affixed. From that point on it would be protected by the seal and by the Roman soldiers.

At this point Jesus' disciples were convinced that their faith in him as the promised Messiah—the Savior of Israel—had been unfounded. He was dead and buried, and with him had been buried the greatest of their hopes and aspirations. The leaders of national Israel had rejected his claim and they themselves could

Prelude to Glory

not dispute the fact that God had allowed him to suffer and die. Surely, had he actually been the Son of God as he had claimed, he would have had the power to save himself, and them, from the Romans, just as Moses had saved their fathers from the Egyptians fifteen hundred years before.

✻ ✻ ✻ ✻ ✻

When the perishable has been clothed with the imperishable, and the mortal with immortality, then the saying that is written will come true:
"Death has been swallowed up in victory."

> Where, O death, is your victory?
> Where O death, is your sting?

The sting of death is sin, and the power of sin is the law. But thanks be to God! He gives us the victory through our Lord Jesus Christ.

I Corinthians 15:54–57

CHAPTER NINE

The Rising of the Son

One of the most difficult sections of the Gospels to harmonize is that of the resurrection day appearances of Jesus and the visits to the tomb. It is important to begin with a consideration of the purpose for which the Gospel accounts of the resurrection were written in the first place. It was not the writers' purpose to provide a chronology of the events surrounding the resurrection. Had it been, we would not have the difficulty we have today in determining that chronology. On the contrary, their purpose was to substantiate the claim that Jesus had risen from the dead. The facts they offered as proof can be listed as follows:

1. Jesus was dead when removed from the cross.
2. The body was placed in a particular tomb.
3. The tomb was sealed and guarded.
4. The tomb was later found to be empty.
5. Jesus was later seen alive by people who knew him.
6. The resurrected body was the same body as the one which had been put to death.

All six of these facts were established beyond a reasonable doubt by the Gospel writers. Each, however, recorded only those events, from the many available, which he felt necessary to substantiate the resurrection. The fact that the writers did not "get their stories together" is, in and of itself, proof that there was no "collusion" among them. The differences in their stories are exactly as seen in courts of law today when different witnesses are called upon to give their versions of an event to which each has been a witness. The subject under consideration must be approached with each individual writer's purpose clearly in mind or the student will immediately become submerged in a myriad of detail, much of which on the surface may appear contradictory.

TESTIMONY REGARDING RESURRECTION

FACT	MATTHEW	MARK	LUKE	JOHN	OTHER
1. That Jesus was dead when removed from the cross.	27: 50-56	15: 37-41	23: 46-49	19: 31-37	I Cor 15: 3
2. That the body was placed in the tomb.	27: 57-61	15: 42-47	23: 50-54	19: 38-56	I Cor 15: 4
3. That the tomb was sealed and guarded.	27: 62-66 28: 4 28: 11-15				
4. That the tomb was later found to be empty.	28: 1-8	16: 1-8	24: 1-8	20: 1-10	I Cor 15: 4
5. That Jesus was later seen alive by people who knew him.	28: 9-10	16: 9; 12-14	24: 13-35	20: 11-18 21: 1-25	I Cor 15: 5-8 Acts 1: 1-11
6. That the resurrected body was the same body as the one which had been put to death.			24: 36-43	20: 19-20 20: 26-31	

The Rising of the Son

Sequence of Appearances

The Gospel writers and Paul (I Cor. 15) give the sequence of Jesus' appearances following his resurrection. Any scenario offered must satisfy this sequence.

1. To Mary Magdalene
2. To the other women
3. To Peter
4. To the two on the road to Emmaus
5. To the apostles (Thomas absent)
6. To the apostles (Thomas present)

The Location(s) of the Disciples

The details of the various accounts make it obvious the disciples were not all staying at the same location. It is commonly believed the Passover meal was celebrated at the home of Mark. This being the case, it is reasonable to assume that, when the disciples were scattered in the Garden of Gethsemane, at least some of them returned to Mark's house and may well have remained in hiding there until Sunday night. The prominence of Mark's house in the book of Acts heightens this possibility.

John 20:2 makes it clear that Peter and John were staying together, possibly at a house owned by John. Additionally, we know from John 19:27 that Jesus' mother was also staying with John. Mary Magdalene; Mary, the mother of James; and Salome, John's mother, also appear to have been staying together. It is likely, therefore, that they all were staying at John's house. There is a strong probability that James and Andrew were there, too.

That the apostles were staying in two separate locations is further supported by the account of the women returning from the tomb to report to them. Notice the following facts which at first seem contradictory but cease to appear so if we assume the apostles were in two different places.

1. The women left the tomb and ran to tell the disciples (Matt. 28:8).
2. Jesus met them en route (Matt. 28:9).
3. They told everything to the eleven (Luke 24:9).
4. However, when the women reported to the disciples in

Luke 24:23, they only reported their conversation with the angels at the tomb who *said* that Jesus was alive. They did not mention actually seeing Jesus themselves, which is inconceivable if they had in fact seen him.

The obvious answer to this difficulty is that they reported to some but not all of the disciples before they met Jesus, then met him while en route to a second location to report to the rest. Thomas and some of the others may have been at still different locations, but we will assume Mark's and John's houses to be the primary locations in the scenario that follows.

The First Visit to the Tomb—Two Women

Matt. 28:1 After the Sabbath, at dawn on the first day of the week, Mary Magdalene and the other Mary went to look at the tomb.

A. T. Robertson, in his book, *Harmony of the Gospels*, translates this passage as follows:

Now *late on the sabbath,* as it began to *draw toward* the first day of the week, came Mary Magdalene and the other Mary to see the sepulchre [italics added].

He provides the following footnote concerning this translation:

This phrase once gave much trouble, but the usage of the vernacular Koine Greek amply justifies the translation. The visit of the women to inspect the tomb was thus made before the sabbath was over (6:00 P.M. on Saturday). The distance was not more than a sabbath day's journey.

Mark 16:1 When the Sabbath was over, Mary Magdalene, Mary the mother of James, and Salome bought spices so that they might go to anoint Jesus' body.

Jesus' body had been hastily buried in a borrowed tomb prior to the onset of the Passover Sabbath. Joseph of Arimathea and

The Rising of the Son

Nicodemus had placed the body in a burial shroud along with seventy-five pounds of spices to keep the body from beginning to smell until they could return and remove it from the temporary tomb. After the Sabbath they obviously intended to prepare the body properly for burial which would require much more time than had previously been available. They would then put it back into the burial shroud and place it in a permanent tomb.

Late on the seventh-day Sabbath the two women visited the tomb. They then returned to the city and, along with Salome, "when the Sabbath was over," bought spices to prepare ointment with which to anoint the body the following morning.

The Resurrection

Matt. 28:2 There was a violent earthquake, for an angel of the Lord came down from heaven and, going to the tomb, rolled back the stone and sat on it.
   3 His appearance was like lightning, and his clothes were white as snow.
   4 The guards were so afraid of him that they shook and became like dead men.

There were no witnesses to the resurrection itself. The combination of the earthquake (the second in the same week) and the appearance of the heavenly messenger was enough to cause these Roman soldiers to literally faint. How long they were out no one knows, but apparently they did wake and return to the city before dawn for there is no mention made by the women of having seen them the next morning. Jesus had stated in the Garden of Gethsemane that he could call down more than twelve legions of angels from heaven for protection had he desired to do so. It is interesting to note that it took only one angel to overcome all the elaborate precautions that the Jews and Romans had taken. Having opened the tomb, the angel took his post atop the stone and waited for the coming morning when the world would receive its Savior from the grave. No one knows at what point in time Jesus broke the bonds of Hades and walked from the tomb, victorious over death. No one needs to. The glory is in the fact, not

Prelude to Glory

the time. The prelude had ended, the risen Son awaited the rising of the sun.

The Second Visit to the Tomb—Three Women

> **Luke 24:1** On the first day of the week, very early in the morning, the women took the spices they had prepared and went to the tomb. (Mark 16:2; John 20:1)
>
> **Mark 16:3** And they asked each other, "Who will roll the stone away from the entrance of the tomb?"
>
> **4** But when they looked up, they saw that the stone, which was very large, had been rolled away. (Luke 24:2)
>
> **Luke 24:3** But when they entered, they did not find the body of the Lord Jesus.

Mary Magdalene; Mary, the mother of James; and Salome had risen while it was yet dark (John 20:1) to go to the tomb to anoint the body of Jesus. They took with them the spices they had prepared the night before. More than likely they left the others at John's house asleep. The trip to the tomb would have taken approximately eighteen to twenty minutes, allowing them to arrive at "early dawn." After looking inside the tomb and finding it empty they assumed someone had arrived before them, possibly Saturday night, and taken the body from its temporary place. In their minds this would also account for the absence of the guards. Consideration of a resurrection was evidently far from their thoughts, and Mary Magdalene went back to John's house to tell him and Peter what they had found. The other two remained at the tomb and probably passed the time by looking around the garden for someone who might know what had happened.

Mary Reports to Peter and John

> **John 20:2** So she came running to Simon Peter and the other disciple, the one Jesus loved, and said, "They have taken the Lord out of the tomb, and we don't know where they have put him!"
>
> **3** So Peter and the other disciple started for the tomb.

The Rising of the Son

Mary affirmed that she had seen the empty tomb and that the body of Jesus was not there. To do this she had to have entered the tomb before reporting to the apostles, even though John does not mention this fact in his Gospel. Further, she made no mention of angels and she certainly would have if she had seen any in or around the tomb. Neither Peter nor John had any knowledge of what might have taken place, but they left immediately to try to find out.

Meanwhile, back in the garden, the women had returned to the tomb from their inspection of the area "after the sun had risen" (Mark 16:2). As they approached the tomb, they were confronted by an angel who informed them of the resurrection and invited them to reinspect the tomb.

The Third Visit to the Tomb—Two Women

Matt. 28:5 The angel said to the women, "Do not be afraid, for I know that you are looking for Jesus, who was crucified.
6 He is not here; he has risen, just as he said. Come and see the place where he lay."
Mark 16:5 As they entered the tomb, they saw a young man dressed in a white robe sitting on the right side, and they were alarmed.
6 "Don't be alarmed," he said. "You are looking for Jesus the Nazarene, who was crucified. He has risen! He is not here. See the place where they laid him."

Upon entering the tomb the women encountered a second angel sitting on the right side of where Jesus had lain. His message was essentially the same as that of the first angel. As the women stood there amazed at what they were seeing, the angel from the outside entered the tomb behind them and they found themselves in the presence of two heavenly beings. It is at this time that the conversation with two angels, as reported by Luke, took place.

Luke 24:4 While they were wondering about this, suddenly two men in clothes that gleamed like lightning stood beside them.

Prelude to Glory

5	In their fright the women bowed down with their faces to the ground, but the men said to them, "Why do you look for the living among the dead?
6	He is not here; he has risen! Remember how he told you, while he was still with you in Galilee:
7	'The Son of Man must be delivered into the hands of sinful men, be crucified and on the third day be raised again.'"
8	Then they remembered his words.
Mark 16:7	"But go, tell his disciples and Peter, 'He is going ahead of you into Galilee. There you will see him, just as he told you.'" (Matt. 28:7)
Matt. 28:8	So the women hurried away from the tomb, afraid yet filled with joy, and ran to tell his disciples. (Mark 16:8)

Jesus intended to spend the last few days before his ascension with his apostles in Galilee. He now sent the message to them to "go to Galilee," where he would meet with them. The same message was later conveyed through the women by Jesus himself, and it is probable that Emmaus, the village where Jesus later dined with two disciples, was on the way to Galilee. The disciples, however, did not heed any of the messages and Jesus himself had to return to Jerusalem to get them to go. Even then, it took two additional appearances over a period of a week to convince all of them that he was alive.

Mary, the mother of James, and Salome knew that Mary Magdalene had gone to tell Peter and John so they evidently went to tell some of the others who they knew were staying at Mark's house. There is no indication that the various people involved in those early morning activities crossed paths as they went from one place to another. The garden itself would probably have had more than one entrance and the north side of the city had several gates which could have been used depending on a person's destination. This, combined with the fact that there were different destinations, easily accounts for the possibility that several people went back and forth without meeting one another. Following the women's departure Peter and John arrived at the tomb with Mary Magdalene trailing behind.

The Rising of the Son

The Fourth Visit to the Tomb—Peter and John

John 20:4 Both were running, but the other disciple outran Peter and reached the tomb first.
   5 He bent over and looked in at the strips of linen lying there but did not go in.
   6 Then Simon Peter, who was behind him, arrived and went into the tomb. He saw the strips of linen lying there,
   7 as well as the burial cloth that had been around Jesus' head. The cloth was folded up by itself, separate from the linen.
   8 Finally the other disciple, who had reached the tomb first, also went inside. He saw and believed.
   9 (They still did not understand from Scripture that Jesus had to rise from the dead.)
   10 Then the disciples went back to their homes.

Mary's early morning announcement had brought these two disciples literally running to the tomb. John was the first to arrive but waited for Peter before entering the tomb. All they found was an empty grave. For some unrecorded reason the angels did not desire to make themselves known to the apostles as they did to Mary Magdalene a few minutes later when she returned to the tomb.

In spite of their boasting at the Passover meal of their willingness to "die with Jesus," the apostles had fled in terror from the Garden of Gethsemane. With the exception of Peter and John who were present at the high priest's palace and later John being with Mary at the cross, they had evidently remained in hiding during the entire time since Jesus' arrest. There is no record of any of the apostles' being present when Jesus' body was removed from the cross or when Joseph and Nicodemus placed it in the tomb. Even as late as Sunday night when the two disciples returned from Emmaus, the apostles were still in hiding "for fear of the Jews."

The women, on the other hand, were present almost continuously from the time Jesus was placed on the cross until his burial. They were the first to return to the tomb on Saturday and again early on Sunday morning. It may have been for this dedication that they were given the honor of being the first to hear the resurrection message and the first to see the resurrected Christ.

For whatever the reason, Peter and John were left with only the articles of burial clothing for which the risen Christ had no further need: the napkin which had been tied around his jaw and the shroud in which the body had rested. They were indeed a confused Peter and John who returned home that morning. Was it still fear that kept them inside their house while the women busily investigated the facts and carried the messages? By the time Peter and John left, Mary had returned to the tomb.

The Risen Christ

The Fifth Visit to the Tomb—Mary Magdalene

John 20:11 But Mary stood outside the tomb crying. As she wept, she bent over to look into the tomb
12 And saw two angels in white, seated where Jesus' body had been, one at the head and the other at the foot.
13 They asked her, "Woman, why are you crying?" "They have taken my Lord away," she said, "and I don't know where they have put him."
14 At this, she turned around and saw Jesus standing there, but she did not realize that it was Jesus. (Mark 16:9)
15 "Woman," he said, "why are you crying? Who is it you are looking for?" Thinking he was the gardener, she said, "Sir, if you have carried him away, tell me where you have put him, and I will get him."
16 Jesus said to her, "Mary." She turned toward him and cried out in Aramaic, "Rabboni!" (which means Teacher).
17 Jesus said, "Do not hold on to me, for I have not yet returned to the Father. Go instead to my brothers and tell them, 'I am returning to my Father and your Father, to my God and your God.'"

The Rising of the Son

An interesting aspect of Jesus' resurrection worth noting at this time is that people did not seem to be able to recognize him. Mary mistook him for a gardener. The two journeying to Emmaus spent considerable time with Jesus without recognizing him. Again, the apostles ate breakfast with Jesus on the shore of the Sea of Galilee but they "dared [not] ask him, 'Who are you?' They knew it was the Lord" (John 21:12). This inability to recognize Jesus was not universal for the group of women seem to have had no such problem, nor did the apostles on Sunday night. The answer appears to be that Jesus could make himself recognizable or unrecognizable at will.

Having seen Jesus in person and knowing that he was alive, Mary left the tomb to report the resurrection to Peter and John.

The Report from the Women

Meanwhile, the other Mary and Salome were carrying their message from the angels to the other disciples. After leaving the tomb they made their way through the streets of Jerusalem just as the shops were beginning to open and the city was coming to life. They went to where they knew some of Jesus' disciples were staying, Mark's house, as has already been discussed. What transpired there was related to Jesus by the two travelers on the way to Emmaus.

> **Luke 24:22** In addition, some of our women amazed us. They went to the tomb early this morning
> **23** But didn't find his body. They came and told us that they had seen a vision of angels, who said he was alive.

This report describes perfectly what happened to Mary, the mother of James, and Salome at the tomb and shows that they were the ones who reported to the disciples at Mark's house. Mary Magdalene could not have been a part of this group—either before or after seeing Jesus. Because Mary had seen Jesus immediately after talking with the angels, there was no point in time when she could have reported seeing the angels but not seeing Jesus. It also shows that the two women reported to at least some of the disciples before seeing Jesus, for if they had met him prior to this they would certainly have mentioned it. This further substantiates the position that all of the disciples were not staying in the same location.

The women then left Mark's house and went to John's house to find Peter and John and any other disciples who might have been staying there. It was probably at Mark's house that Joanna and some of the other women joined the two who had been at the tomb.

The Sixth Visit to the Tomb—the Delegation

As the women left Mark's house, the brethren there sent a delegation to the tomb to verify what the women had said.

> **Luke 24:24** Then some of our companions went to the tomb and found it just as the women had said, but him they did not see.

No indication is given whereby we might know if this delegation saw any angels or just the empty tomb. They certainly did not see Jesus.

The Women Meet Jesus on the Road

> **Matt. 28:9** Suddenly Jesus met them. "Greetings," he said. They came to him, clasped his feet and worshiped him.
> **10** Then Jesus said to them, "Do not be afraid. Go and tell my brothers to go to Galilee; there they will see me."

Jesus met these women as they were traveling from one group of disciples to another. The message he gave them was the same one given earlier by the angels in the tomb; "Go to Galilee." As these women continued in search of the other disciples, the soldiers who had been assigned to guard the tomb were at the temple reporting events to the chief priests and elders who had been hurriedly assembled to deal with this latest crisis.

The Rising of the Son

The Guards Report to the Chief Priest

Matt. 28:11 While the women were on their way, some of the guards went into the city and reported to the chief priests everything that had happened.

12 When the chief priests had met with the elders and devised a plan, they gave the soldiers a large sum of money,

13 telling them, "You are to say, 'His disciples came during the night and stole him away while we were asleep.'

14 "If this report gets to the governor, we will satisfy him and keep you out of trouble."

15 So the soldiers took the money and did as they were instructed. And this story has been widely circulated among the Jews to this very day.

The Roman soldiers in this instance had no little cause for concern. Indeed, sleeping on watch was an offense punishable by

An Empire Builder's Arms & Armor

death. Yet, who would believe their story if they tried to explain what had really happened that night? The Roman authorities would not be likely to believe a story regarding angels, and *fear* was a word supposedly absent from a Roman soldier's vocabulary. It is not clear just when these men "woke up" from having "become as dead men," but it must have been before the women arrived at the tomb early that Sunday morning—which helps us fix the time of the resurrection.

There is no indication that anything had happened before the women went to the tomb late on the Sabbath. Further, we can logically assume that due to the severity of the problem these soldiers were now facing, they would have gone to the Jewish authorities for help as soon as possible. It is obvious they did not want the Roman authorities, and the governor in particular, to learn of the situation. Their only hope was the cooperation of the Jewish authorities who had requested the guard in the first place. The fact that the soldiers waited until morning to report to the chief priests indicates it was probably very late when the earthquake happened and the angel appeared—so late, in fact, that they did not wish to disturb the chief priests at that late hour. Thus, the resurrection, which followed the arrival of the angel, must have been very late at night, or even in the early hours of the morning. Add to this the fact that the story they were told to use (that the body was stolen while they slept) demonstrates that it happened late at night or early in the morning. Mark says it was early on the first day of the week. This terminology represents morning, not evening. The weight of evidence favors an early morning resurrection.

The soldiers probably found some place to spend the balance of the night, then at a decent hour sought out the Jewish authorities to solicit their help. They first contacted a chief priest, probably the one who originally requested that the tomb be guarded. He, upon hearing their report, sent for other chief priests and elders that they might determine the best course of action. This took some period of time which means it was around eight o'clock in the morning when the conversation took place. The decision having been reached, the soldiers were paid "hush money" which must have been considerable, since, as mentioned, sleeping on watch carried the death penalty. Meanwhile, the women arrived at John's house.

The Rising of the Son

The Women Report to Peter and John

The women had been told by the angels to report to the disciples "and Peter." Their first report to the disciples would have satisfied the first directive but they still had the command to "tell Peter."

> **Luke 24:9** When they came back from the tomb, they told all these things to the Eleven and to all the others.
> **10** It was Mary Magdalene, Joanna, Mary the mother of James, and the others with them who told this to the apostles. (Mark 16:10; John 20:18)
> **11** But they did not believe the women, because their words seemed to them like nonsense. (Mark 16:11)

Mary had evidently arrived at John's house about the same time as the other women. Everyone seems to have been present when the report of the angel's message and of the women's seeing Jesus were made to the apostles. While the men were not ready to accept these reports, Peter was sufficiently aroused to cause him to make a second trip to the tomb.

The Seventh Visit to the Tomb—Peter

> **Luke 24:12** Peter, however, got up and ran to the tomb. Bending over, he saw the strips of linen lying by themselves, and he went away, wondering to himself what had happened.

That this was not the same trip to the tomb which Peter had made earlier can be shown from the fact that, on the first trip, Peter entered the tomb along with John, whereas this time he only stooped and looked in. Nothing seemed to have changed so he left the tomb and returned home still perplexed about what had happened. Both Paul (I Cor. 15) and Luke (24:35) tell us that Jesus appeared to Peter on that first Sunday. The appearance was after he appeared to the women but before he appeared to the apostles that night. Therefore, it could have been anytime after Peter left the tomb for the second time up until the apostles gathered for a meal that night. While it would be impossible to fix the exact time,

Prelude to Glory

it is entirely conceivable that it was on this occasion, while Peter was alone, that Jesus chose to make himself known to the apostle. This would also serve to alleviate Peter's mind, which must have been in considerable agony ever since his denials in the court of the high priest. Thus Peter would become the first of the apostles to witness the resurrected Christ.

Two on the Road to Emmaus

Two of the disciples left Jerusalem some time after the delegation returned from the tomb. They had evidently been at Mark's house because they heard the report of the women as well as that of the delegation returning from the tomb. When they left the city for the walk to the village of Emmaus they knew that things had been going on for the past several days that were totally beyond their comprehension. They had seen a man who some thought to be the Messiah crucified and buried. They had witnessed two earthquakes and seen it become dark for three hours in the middle of the day. The temple had been shaken and the great veil destroyed. Women had come in saying they had talked with angels. They may very well have seen people they knew to be dead and buried walking the streets of Jerusalem (Matt. 27:52). Thus it is easy to imagine their amazement when they were joined on the road by a traveler, also from Jerusalem, who apparently knew nothing of these activities.

Luke 24:13 Now that same day two of them were going to a village called Emmaus, about seven miles from Jerusalem.
 14 They were talking with each other about everything that had happened.
 15 As they talked and discussed these things with each other, Jesus himself came up and walked along with them; (Mark 16:12)
 16 but they were kept from recognizing him.
 17 He asked them, "What are you discussing together as you walk along?" They stood still, their faces downcast.
 18 One of them, named Cleopas, asked him, "Are

The Rising of the Son

you only a visitor to Jerusalem and do not know the things that have happened there in these days?"

19 "What things?" he asked. "About Jesus of Nazareth," they replied. "He was a prophet, powerful in word and deed before God and all the people.

20 The chief priests and our rulers handed him over to be sentenced to death, and they crucified him;

21 but we had hoped that he was the one who was going to redeem Israel. And what is more, it is the third day since all this took place.

22 In addition, some of our women amazed us. They went to the tomb early this morning

23 but didn't find his body. They came and told us that they had seen a vision of angels, who said he was alive.

24 Then some of our companions went to the tomb and found it just as the women had said, but him they did not see."

25 He said to them, "How foolish you are, and how slow of heart to believe all that the prophets have spoken!

26 Did not the Christ have to suffer these things and then enter his glory?"

27 And beginning with Moses and all the Prophets, he explained to them what was said in all the Scriptures concerning himself.

28 As they approached the village to which they were going, Jesus acted as if he were going farther.

29 But they urged him strongly, "Stay with us, for it is nearly evening; the day is almost over." So he went in to stay with them.

30 When he was at the table with them, he took bread, gave thanks, broke it and began to give it to them.

31 Then their eyes were opened and they recognized him, and he disappeared from their sight.

> 32 They asked each other, "Were not our hearts burning within us while he talked with us on the road and opened the Scriptures to us?"
> 33a They got up and returned at once to Jerusalem.

There has been considerable speculation about who these two disciples were. One is named by Luke and some have theorized that the other was Peter; this being the appearance mentioned by Paul in I Corinthians 15. The context does not support this position, however, as the travelers stated in verse twenty-four that "some of our *companions* went to the tomb." Since Peter went to the tomb and these two did not, there is no way one of them could have been Peter. There can be no doubt, however, that they were disciples and were fully aware of the activities that had been going on. This is further indicated by the fact that upon returning to Jerusalem they knew exactly where to find the apostles.

Jesus and the two disciples arrived at Emmaus late in the day and initially planned to spend the night there. At the evening meal, however, their eyes were opened and they recognized Jesus. They considered this revelation too important to wait until morning so they rose and returned to Jerusalem. The return trip would have taken about three hours which would have put them back at Mark's house sometime between eight and nine in the evening. This corresponds with John's statement that it was on the evening of the first day of the week (Roman time).

The Appearance to the Apostles—Thomas Absent

> **Luke 24:33b** There they found the Eleven and those with them, assembled together
> 34 and saying, "It is true! The Lord has risen and has appeared to Simon."
> 35 Then the two told what had happened on the way, and how Jesus was recognized by them when he broke the bread. (Mark 16:13)

The two from Emmaus found all the apostles together with the exception of Thomas. By this time, Peter's testimony had been added to that of the women. Evidently some disciples were still

The Rising of the Son

skeptical, even after the travelers from Emmaus added their story. While they were talking, Jesus himself appeared in the room with them.

John 20:19 On the evening of that first day of the week, when the disciples were together, with the doors locked for fear of the Jews, Jesus came and stood among them and said, "Peace be with you!" (Mark 16:14; Luke 24:36)

Luke 24:37 They were startled and frightened, thinking they saw a ghost.

38 He said to them, "Why are you troubled, and why do doubts rise in your minds?"

Mark 16:14 . . . he rebuked them for their lack of faith and their stubborn refusal to believe those who had seen him after he had risen.

Luke 24:39 "Look at my hands and my feet. It is I myself! Touch me and see; a ghost does not have flesh and bones, as you see I have."

40 When he had said this, he showed them his hands and feet. (John 20:20)

41 And while they still did not believe it because of joy and amazement, he asked them, "Do you have anything here to eat?"

42 They gave him a piece of broiled fish,

43 and he took it and ate it in their presence.

Following his resurrection Jesus apparently had the ability to manifest himself at will and then disappear when he so chose. Thus he disappeared before the disciples at Emmaus and was able to appear in the midst of the apostles, even though they were meeting behind locked doors. This method of appearing no doubt added to the amazement that would have resulted from seeing him alive in the flesh.

Jesus seemed to have felt that they should have known he would be resurrected, and he upbraided them for their reluctance to accept the word of their brethren. The fact that they were still in Jerusalem after receiving clear instructions to go to Galilee must have added to his disappointment in them. Nevertheless, Jesus

Prelude to Glory

used the occasion to give to the apostles the first of three recorded commissions regarding their work in the days ahead.

The First Commission

> **John 20:21** Again Jesus said, "Peace be with you! As the Father has sent me, I am sending you."
> 22 And with that he breathed on them and said, "Receive the Holy Spirit.
> 23 If you forgive anyone his sins, they are forgiven; if you do not forgive them, they are not forgiven."

In the days to come, while walking along the shores of the Sea of Galilee and again upon returning to Jerusalem prior to his ascension, this basic commission would be enlarged upon. The apostles did not receive the Holy Spirit at this time but were only given a brief summary of their work which would begin when they did receive it. Jesus still had forty days left upon the earth during which to complete the training of the men who would establish his church. The apostles had had about all they could absorb for one day. Additional instructions would have to wait for another day and place. Besides, Thomas, one of the eleven, was not present and he, too, would participate in the training.

> **John 20:24** Now Thomas (called Didymus), one of the Twelve, was not with the disciples when Jesus came.
> 25 When the other disciples told him, that they had seen the Lord, he declared, "Unless I see the nail marks in his hands and put my fingers where the nails were, and put my hands into his side, I will not believe it."

The Appearance to the Apostles—Thomas Present

A week later the apostles were still in Jerusalem. Thomas had refused to believe the reports in spite of the number of witnesses now testifying to the resurrection. Fear was still a controlling force as once again we find the apostles behind closed doors in what was probably the same location as before. Jesus displayed his

The Rising of the Son

continuing patience as once again he appeared to them, this time for the specific benefit of Thomas.

> **John 20:26** A week later his disciples were in the house again, and Thomas was with them. Though the doors were locked, Jesus came and stood among them and said, "Peace be with you!"
> **27** Then he said to Thomas, "Put your finger here; see my hands. Reach out your hand and put it into my side. Stop doubting and believe."
> **28** Thomas said to him, "My Lord and my God!"

Now, even doubting Thomas was forced to believe and thus the college of apostles was complete. Two others would be added later who are outside the scope of this work, but the original eleven had now all been brought into a state of belief.

> **John 20:29** Then Jesus told him, "Because you have seen me, you have believed; blessed are those who have not seen and yet have believed."

* * * * *

That which was from the beginning, which we have heard, which we have seen with our eyes, which we have looked at and our hands have touched—this we proclaim concerning the word of life. The life appeared; we have seen it and testify to it, and we proclaim to you the eternal life, which was with the Father and has appeared to us.

I John 1:1–2

CHAPTER TEN

The Last Forty Days

Jesus apparently adhered to the tradition of leaving Jerusalem and going home for the harvest season before returning for the celebration of Pentecost. Most pilgrims would have remained in Jerusalem for the duration of the Feast of Unleavened Bread which would have run through the twenty-first of Nisan. We know that Jesus and his disciples remained in Jerusalem for the week after his resurrection which would have put them leaving for Galilee at about the same time as the last of the pilgrims.

Acts 1:3 states that Jesus remained on the earth for forty days following his resurrection. We are told very little about those forty days, but it appears from the context that most of Christ's time was spent in Galilee. It was here that Jesus made his third appearance to the apostles.

The Return to Galilee

It was entirely fitting that Jesus would spend his last days on earth in the quiet countryside of Galilee. He had been brought there by his parents as a young child and it was there he had grown to manhood and begun his ministry. All of the apostles, with the exception of Judas, were Galilean. Jesus' first miracle had been performed at Cana of Galilee. The Sermon on the Mount had been preached and the five thousand fed in Galilee. In fact, the majority of Jesus' ministry had been conducted in Galilee.

Galilee was a rural province by and large. Although there were cities such as Capernaum, basically this area was the farmland of Palestine. Much of the food grown here wound up on the tables in Jerusalem. The Jordan river also had its source there, and the Sea of Galilee provided such excellent fishing that Peter and John were

The Last Forty Days

Fishermen on Sea of Galilee

Prelude to Glory

A view of (above) and from (below) the Sea of Galilee.

Galilee: Homeland of Jesus

The Last Forty Days

"The grass withers, and the flower falls, but the world of the Lord abides for ever" (I Pet. 1:24-25). The abundant flowers of the Galilean landscape where Jesus walked and preached (above).

A vew from the western shore of the Sea of Galilee (left).

Prelude to Glory

Mt. Tabor, the traditional site of Jesus' transfiguration (above).
The Sea of Galilee (below) where Jesus taught and performed several miracles.

The Last Forty Days

just two among many who made their livelihood from it. There Jesus provided the final training for the men who established his church.

Scripture tells us very little about those final days in Galilee. Only two events during this period are mentioned by the Gospel writers, a private appearance to the eleven apostles and a public appearance to more than five hundred people.

Jesus Third Appearance to the Apostles

John 21:1 Afterward Jesus appeared again to his disciples by the Sea of Tiberias [Galilee]). It happened in this way:
   2 Simon Peter, Thomas (called Didymus), Nathanael from Cana in Galilee, the sons of Zebedee, and two other disciples were together.
   3 "I'm going out to fish," Simon Peter told them, and they said, "We'll go with you." So they went out and got into the boat, but that night they caught nothing.
   4 Early in the morning, Jesus stood on the shore, but the disciples did not realize that it was Jesus.
   5 He called out to them, "Friends, haven't you any fish?" "No," they answered.
   6 He said, "Throw your net on the right side of the boat and you will find some." When they did, they were unable to haul the net in because of the large number of fish.
   7 Then the disciple whom Jesus loved said to Peter, "It is the Lord!" As soon as Simon Peter heard him say, "It is the Lord," he wrapped his outer garment around him (for he had taken it off) and jumped into the water.
   8 The other disciples followed in the boat, towing the net full of fish, for they were not far from shore, about a hundred yards.
   9 When they landed, they saw a fire of burning coals there with fish on it, and some bread.

10 Jesus said to them, "Bring some of the fish you have just caught."
11 Simon Peter climbed aboard and dragged the net ashore. It was full of large fish, 153, but even with so many the net was not torn.
12 Jesus said to them, "Come and have breakfast." None of the disciples dared ask him, "Who are you?" They knew it was the Lord.
13 Jesus came, and took the bread and gave it to them, and did the same with the fish.
14 This was now the third time Jesus appeared to his disciples after he was raised from the dead.

Again, the disciples had difficulty recognizing Jesus. John seemed to realize it was Jesus from the miraculous catch of fish and when he said so the others came to the same realization. Jesus used the occasion to further his teaching.

John 21:15 When they had finished eating, Jesus said to Simon Peter, "Simon son of John, do you truly love me more than these?" "Yes, Lord," he said, "you know that I love you." Jesus said, "Feed my lambs."
16 Again Jesus said, "Simon son of John, do you truly love me?" He answered, "Yes Lord, you know that I love you." Jesus said, "Take care of my sheep."
17 The third time he said to him, "Simon son of John, do you love me?" Peter was hurt because Jesus asked him the third time, "Do you love me?" He said, "Lord, you know all things; you know that I love you." Jesus said, "Feed my sheep."

At the Passover supper Peter had bragged that he had the courage to follow Jesus even into death. Barely hours later he was denying with an oath that he had ever known him. Just as he had denied him three times, Jesus seemed now to require that Peter affirm him three times. Peter did so, as he had affirmed him before. But this time there was a difference. The difference was

The Last Forty Days

the resurrection. Peter would never again deny his Lord. All of the apostles had run away that night in Gethsemane. None of them would ever run again. And Jesus used the occasion to let Peter know what lay ahead of him as he carried out the commission to preach to the entire world.

> **John 21:18** "I tell you the truth, when you were younger you dressed yourself and went where you wanted; but when you are old you will stretch out your hands, and someone else will dress you and lead you where you do not want to go."
> **19** Jesus said this to indicate the kind of death by which Peter would glorify God. Then he said to him, "Follow me!"

Having been told this, Peter asked, "What about John?" This is a typical reaction to being told something not completely to one's liking. As the old saying goes, misery loves company. Jesus' answer to this was a mild rebuke. Peter was told to worry about himself and let Jesus worry about John and the others.

> **John 21:20** Peter turned and saw that the disciple whom Jesus loved was following them. (This was the one who had leaned backed against Jesus at the supper and had said, "Lord, who is going to betray you?")
> **21** When Peter saw him, he asked, "Lord, what about him?"
> **22** Jesus answered, "If I want him to remain alive until I return, what is that to you? You must follow me."

At the Passover supper Jesus had told Peter, "Where I am going you cannot follow now, but you will follow later" (John 13:36). Jesus was referring to the cross. Peter's subsequent denials proved that Jesus was right in his assessment of Peter's faith at that time. Now he told him that he would follow.

Again, in John 14:3 Jesus spoke of going to prepare a place for the disciples; then having done so, returning to take them to be with him. Many believe these passages refer to Jesus' going to heaven to prepare a place for humanity. This cannot be inasmuch as Matthew 25:34 clearly states that heaven has been prepared and waiting for us since before the creation of the world. In all these references Jesus was actually talking about the cross. It was on the cross that he prepared a place in heaven for mankind. Had Jesus not gone to the cross, heaven would have still existed, but there would have been no place there for sinful man. It was also to a cross that Jesus consigned Peter.

Jesus' statement in verse twenty-two evidently caused a rumor to be started that the apostle John would not die. Before concluding his Gospel, John corrects this rumor.

> **John 21:23** Because of this, the rumor spread among the brothers that this disciple would not die. But Jesus did not say that he would not die; he only said, "If I want him to remain alive until I return, what is that to you?"

The End of John's Gospel

It is at this point that the apostle John closes his Gospel. Irenaeus, the pupil of Polycarp who was a friend and pupil of the apostle, wrote that John "for sixty years after the ascension preached orally, till the end of Domitian's reign; and after the death of Domitian having returned to Ephesus, he was induced to write [his Gospel] concerning the divinity of Christ."

This dates John's Gospel more than a generation after the other Gospels, indicating that the life and labors of Jesus were by this time well known to Christians. In the meantime the apostles had preached the Gospel to the entire creation (Col. 1:23), Paul and Peter had suffered martyrdom, all the other apostles had passed to their reward, and Jerusalem had been destroyed.

> **John 21:24** This is the disciple who testifies to these things and who wrote them down. We know that his testimony is true.
> **25** Jesus did many other things as well. If every one of them were written down, I suppose that even the whole world would not have room for the books that would be written.

The Last Forty Days
The Great Commission

The next event during the forty-day period recorded by the Gospel writers was Jesus' public appearance to some five hundred people on a mountain in Galilee. The apostle Paul also referred to this meeting in his first letter to the church at Corinth. In this instance, Jesus talked about his church, and gave what has come to be known as the Great Commission.

> **Matt. 28:16** Then the eleven disciples went to Galilee, to the mountain where Jesus had told them to go.
>
> **I Cor. 15:6** After that, he appeared to more than five hundred of the brothers at the same time, most of whom are still living, though some have fallen asleep.
>
> **Matt. 28:17** When they saw him, they worshiped him; but some doubted.

Matthew 28:17 shows that more than just the eleven were present at the event described. All of the eleven apostles had been brought to a state of belief prior to this meeting, but others obviously continued to have doubts. This appearance by Jesus would have removed those doubts. Paul mentions an appearance to more than five hundred and this was evidently when it happened. Thus, five hundred more witnesses saw the resurrected Christ.

The apostles had a particular function in establishing the church. That function was of limited duration, and consequently, there are no apostles today. There was a greater commission for the church, however. The Great Commission applies to every Christian at every time and in every place. It is in fact the most explicit statement of the purpose of the church that has ever been made.

> **Matt. 28:18** Then Jesus came to them and said, "All authority in heaven and on earth has been given to me."
>
> **Mark 16:15** He said to them, "Go into all the world and preach the good news to all creation."
>
> **Matt. 28:19** ". . . and make disciples of all nations, baptizing

them in the name of the Father and of the Son and of the Holy Spirit.

20 And teaching them to obey everything I have commanded you. And surely I am with you always, to the very end of the age."

Mark 16:16 "Whoever believes and is baptized will be saved, but whoever does not believe will be condemned."

In addition to giving the multitude the commission, Jesus told them certain signs would be a part of the church during the first century. Notice that these were not abilities given to those who believed but rather were to "accompany" those who believed. These same phenomena were a part of the giving of the Law of Moses as well. Both Moses and Aaron were given the ability to confirm their teaching with miracles. Thus the apostles would be aided in establishing the church with the ability to confirm their words with signs. Paul states unequivocally that these signs would pass away (I Cor. 13).

Mark 16:17 And these signs will accompany those who believe: In my name they will drive out demons; they will speak in new tongues;

18 they will pick up snakes with their hands; and when they drink deadly poison, it will not hurt them at all; they will place their hands on sick people, and they will get well.

The End of Matthew's Gospel

According to Papias and Irenaeus, Matthew wrote an Aramaic Gospel, traces of which, however, have never been discovered. There is nothing about the Greek Gospel of Matthew to indicate it is a translation from an Aramaic original. Because Greek was generally spoken in Palestine and Matthew's occupation would require that he be familiar with that language, it is much more probable that this Gospel is a Greek original than a translation of a former Aramaic Gospel.

The Last Forty Days

Irenaeus, who lived in the second century, says it was written "when Peter and Paul were preaching at Rome." This would date it later than A.D. 61 and it is evident from the Gospel itself that it was written prior to the destruction of Jerusalem (A.D. 70). Matthew's Gospel was generally believed by the church fathers to be the first of the four written.

The End of Mark's Gospel

Mark ends his Gospel with the words:

Mark 16:19 After the Lord Jesus had spoken to them, he was taken up into heaven and he sat at the right hand of God.
20 Then the disciples went out and preached everywhere, and the Lord worked with them and confirmed his word by the signs that accompanied it.

John Mark was the son of Mary, a Christian Jewess, in whose home the early Christians seem to have been sheltered (Acts 12:12). He was peculiarly Roman in his training and development. He was either the nephew or cousin of Barnabas and accompanied him and Paul on their first missionary journey. Because Mark left them at Perga, Paul objected when Barnabas proposed that Mark accompany them on their second journey. The result was that Silas was Paul's companion, not Barnabas. That friendly relations between Paul and Mark were afterwards resumed is evident from the fact that he was with Paul during Paul's first imprisonment (Col. 4:10).

The fact that Mark was with Paul in Rome at the time of his first imprisonment (A.D. 62–63) accords with the tradition that his Gospel was written in that city. He had been with Peter in A.D. 62. From the time of Papias the view has been that Peter supplied Mark with many of the facts from Jesus' life and, according to Clement of Alexandria, Eusebius said the Gospel was submitted to Peter for his approval. This would lead to the conclusion that this Gospel was written between A.D. 63–66 since we are certain it was written prior to the destruction of Jerusalem.

Prelude to Glory
The Final Commission

Only Luke records the final days of Jesus upon the earth. Just prior to Pentecost Jesus led the apostles back to Jerusalem where he spent the last few days with them. Somewhere within the city, possibly at Mark's house, Jesus met with them for the last time.

Luke 24:44 He said to them, "This is what I told you while I was still with you: Everything must be fulfilled that is written about me in the Law of Moses, the Prophets and the Psalms."
45 Then he opened their minds so that they could understand the Scriptures.
46 He told them, "This is what is written: The Christ will suffer and rise from the dead on the third day,
47 And repentance and forgiveness of sins will be preached in his name to all nations, beginning at Jerusalem."
Acts 1:4b ". . . . Do not leave Jerusalem, but wait for the gift my Father promised, which you have heard me speak about.
5 For John baptized with water, but in a few days you will be baptized with the Holy Spirit."
Luke 24:48 "You are witnesses of these things.
49 I am going to send you what my Father has promised; but stay in the city until you have been clothed with power from on high."
50 When he had led them out to the vicinity of Bethany, he lifted up his hands and blessed them.

Jesus limited this final commission to the apostles. His admonition to them to remain in Jerusalem until they received the power from on high precluded its being applicable to any persons today.

The End of Luke's Gospel

Luke 24:51 While he was blessing them, he left them and was taken up into heaven.

The Last Forty Days

52 Then they worshiped him and returned to Jerusalem with great joy.
53 And they stayed continually at the temple, praising God.

Luke was Paul's companion from Troas to Philippi on the second missionary journey (Acts 16:10–17). He later rejoined Paul and stayed with him to the close of the Acts account about A.D. 58 to 63. In II Timothy 4:11 Paul mentions that Luke was with him during his second imprisonment in Rome.

The date of Luke's Gospel is placed immediately before Acts, of which he was also the author and which was addressed to the same individual, Theophilus. Scholars believe Luke wrote it in Rome in A.D. 63. Origen declares that this Gospel was written for the Greeks who had espoused the Christian faith.

The Ascension

The details of the ascension are not recorded in any of the Gospels. Luke, however, does give us the details in the first chapter of Acts. Jesus ascended to heaven a few days before Peter preached the first sermon on Pentecost. The site where Jesus last set foot on the earth was the Mount of Olives.

Acts 1:6 So when they met together, they asked him, "Lord, are you at this time going to restore the kingdom to Israel?"
7 He said to them: "It is not for you to know the times or dates the Father has set by his own authority.
8 But you will receive power when the Holy Spirit comes on you; and you will be my witness in Jerusalem, and in all Judea and Samaria, and to the ends of the earth."
9 After he said this, he was taken up before their very eyes, and a cloud hid him from their sight.
10 They were looking intently up into the sky as he was going, when suddenly two men dressed in white stood beside them.

Prelude to Glory

11 "Men of Galilee," they said, "why do you stand here looking into the sky? This same Jesus, who has been taken from you into heaven, will come back in the same way you have seen him go into heaven."

12 Then they returned to Jerusalem from the hill called the Mount of Olives, a Sabbath day's walk from the city.

13 When they arrived, they went upstairs to the room where they were staying. Those present were Peter, John, James and Andrew; Philip and Thomas, Bartholomew and Matthew; James son of Alphaeus and Simon the Zealot, and Judas son of James.

14 They all joined together constantly in prayer, along with the women and Mary the mother of Jesus, and his brothers.

* * * * *

In my vision at night I looked, and there before me was one like a son of man, coming with the clouds of heaven. He approached the Ancient of Days and was led into his presence. He was given authority, glory and sovereign power; all peoples, nations and men of every language worshiped him. His dominion is an everlasting dominion that will not pass away, and his kingdom is one that will never be destroyed.

Daniel 7:13–14

APPENDIX A

A History of the Passover

The Original Passover

The LORD said to Moses and Aaron in Egypt, "This month is to be for you the first month, the first month of your year. Tell the whole community of Israel that on the *tenth day of this month* each man is to take a lamb for his family, one for each household. If any household is too small for a whole lamb, they must share one with their nearest neighbor, having taken into account the number of people there are. You are to determine the amount of lamb needed in accordance with what each person will eat. The animals you choose must be year-old males without defect, and you may take them from the sheep or the goats. Take care of them until the *fourteenth day of the month,* when all the people of the community of Israel must slaughter them at *twilight.* Then they are to take some of the blood and put it on the sides and tops of the doorframes of the houses where they eat the lambs. That *same night* they are to eat the meat roasted over the fire, along with bitter herbs, and bread made without yeast. Do not eat the meat raw or cooked in water, but roast it over the fire—head, legs and inner parts. Do not leave any of it till morning; if some is left till morning, you must burn it. This is how you are to eat it: with your cloak tucked into your belt, your sandals on your feet and your staff in your hand. Eat it in haste; it is the LORD's *Passover.*

"On that *same night* I will pass through Egypt and strike down every firstborn—both men and animals—and I will bring judgment on all the gods of Egypt. I am the LORD. The blood will be a sign for you on the houses where you are; and when I see the blood, I will pass over you. No destructive plague will touch you when I strike Egypt." (Exod. 12:1–13, italics added)

Moses Instructs the People

Then Moses summoned all the elders of Israel and said to them, "Go at once and select the animals for your families and slaughter the Passover lamb. Take a bunch of hyssop, dip it into the blood in the basin and put some of the blood on the top and on both sides of the doorframe. Not one of you shall go out the door of his house until morning. When the LORD goes through the land to strike down the Egyptians, he will see the blood on the top and sides of the doorframe and will pass over that doorway, and he will not permit the destroyer to enter your houses and strike you down.

"Obey these instructions as a lasting ordinance for you and your descendants. When you enter the land that the LORD will give you as he promised, observe this ceremony. And when your children ask you 'What does this ceremony mean to you?' then tell them, 'It is the Passover sacrifice to the LORD, who passed over the houses of the Israelites in Egypt and spared our homes when he struck down the Egyptians.'" Then the people bowed down and worshiped. The Israelites did just what the Lord commanded Moses and Aaron. (Exod. 12:21–28)

The Night of the Passover

At midnight the LORD struck down all the firstborn in Egypt, from the firstborn of Pharaoh, who sat on the throne, to the firstborn of the prisoner, who was in the dungeon, and the firstborn of all the livestock as well. Pharaoh and all his officials and all the Egyptians got up *during the night,* and there was loud wailing in Egypt, for there was not a house without someone dead.

During the night Pharaoh summoned Moses and Aaron and said, "Up! Leave my people, you and the Israelites! Go, worship the LORD as you have requested. Take your flocks and herds, as you have said, and go. And also bless me."

The Egyptians urged the people to hurry and leave the country. "For otherwise," they said, "we will all die!" So the people took their dough before the yeast was added, and carried it on their shoulders in kneading troughs wrapped in clothing. The Israelites did as Moses instructed and asked the Egyptians for articles of silver and gold and for clothing. The LORD had made the Egyptians favorably disposed toward the people, and they gave them what they asked for; so they plundered the Egyptians.

The Israelites journeyed from Rameses to Succoth. There were about six hundred thousand men on foot, besides women and children. Many other people went up with them, as well as large droves of livestock, both flocks and herds. With the dough they had brought from Egypt, they baked cakes of unleavened bread.

Appendix A—A History of the Passover

The dough was without yeast because they had been driven out of Egypt and did not have time to prepare food for themselves. (Exod. 12:29–39, italics added)

Points of Importance

The above scriptures tell the story of the Israelites' departure from Egypt, starting with the first instructions God gave Moses until the people were actually on their way to the Red Sea. In order to properly understand subsequent celebrations of this event, several facts need to be noticed at the outset.

First, the Passover lamb was to be slaughtered and the meal eaten on the *fourteenth of Nisan*. The term *at twilight* in Hebrew literally means, "between the evenings," which describes the time between sunset and the appearance of the "first three stars of evening." The Jewish day began with the setting of the sun. Thus, "between the evenings" referred to the first three hours of the day. This fact will have considerable significance when we study the changes the Jewish leaders had made in the Passover celebration by the time of Jesus.

Second, it was at midnight on that same day, the fourteenth of Nisan, that the Lord struck down all the firstborn in Egypt, and at morning of that same day, the Exodus began. Thus, all of the above described events took place within a twenty-four hour period.

Third, there were three components of the meal: the lamb, the unleavened bread, and the bitter herbs. There is no mention of wine in the first Passover account.

Finally, the meal was eaten before midnight and nothing was allowed to remain until morning. What was left till morning was burned. The people were assembled early in the morning as a result of the instructions which Pharaoh had given to Moses "during the night." It was intended from the beginning that this event would be commemorated as an annual celebration.

The First Celebration

The LORD spoke to Moses in the Desert of Sinai in the first month of the second year after they came out of Egypt. He said,

"Have the Israelites celebrate the Passover at the appointed time. Celebrate it at the appointed time, at *twilight* on the *fourteenth* day of this month, in accordance with all its rules and regulations."

So Moses told the Israelites to celebrate the Passover, and they did so in the Desert of Sinai at *twilight* on the *fourteenth* day of the first month. The Israelites did everything just as the LORD commanded Moses. (Num. 9:1–5, italics added)

The Second Month Passover

But some of them could not celebrate the Passover on that day because they were ceremonially unclean on account of a dead body. So they came to Moses and Aaron that same day and said to Moses, "We have become unclean because of a dead body, but why should we be kept from presenting the LORD's offering with the other Israelites at the appointed time?"

Moses answered them, "Wait until I find out what the Lord commands concerning you."

Then the LORD said to Moses, "Tell the Israelites: 'When any of you or your descendants are unclean because of a dead body or are away on a journey, they may still celebrate the LORD's Passover. They are to celebrate it on the fourteenth day of the second month at twilight. They are to eat the lamb, together with unleavened bread and bitter herbs. They must not leave any of it till morning or break any of its bones. When they celebrate the Passover, they must follow all the regulations. But if a man who is ceremonially clean and not on a journey fails to celebrate the Passover, that person must be cut off from his people because he did not present the LORD's offering at the appointed time. That man will bear the consequences of his sin.

An alien living among you who wants to celebrate the LORD's Passover must do so in accordance with its rules and regulations. You must have the same regulations for the alien and the native-born.'" (Num. 9:6–14)

Points of Importance

There is no mention of the Feast of Unleavened Bread in connection with the celebration of the Passover at Sinai. This is due to the fact that while the Feast of Unleavened Bread is mentioned in Exodus twelve, it is done so with explicit directions:

Appendix A—A History of the Passover

When the LORD brings you into the land of the Canaanites, Hittites . . . you are to observe this ceremony in this month. (Exod. 13:5)

The meal to be eaten at Sinai was essentially the same as that at the original Passover and wine still was not a part of that meal. The meal was to be eaten at twilight on the fourteenth, just as had the original meal. All other requirements appear to have been the same with two exceptions. There was no requirement of putting the blood on the door, and there were provisions added for those who were ceremonially unclean or on a journey. No other mention is made of a celebration of a Passover until just before the leadership of the Israelite nation was turned over to Joshua.

Joshua's Passover

Then the LORD said to Joshua, "Today I have rolled away the reproach of Egypt from you." So the place has been called Gilgal to this day.

On the evening of the fourteenth day of the month, while camped at Gilgal on the plains of Jericho, the Israelites celebrated the Passover. The day after the Passover, that very day, they ate some of the produce of the land: unleavened bread and roasted grain. The manna stopped the day after they ate this food from the land; there was no longer any manna for the Israelites but that year they ate of the produce of Canaan. (Josh. 5:9–12)

Beginning with the twelfth chapter of Deuteronomy God gave to Moses a series of laws to be observed by the Israelites upon entering the "promised land." In chapter sixteen details were given for the celebration of the Passover.

Observe the month of Abib [Nisan] and celebrate the Passover of the LORD your God, because in the month of Abib he brought you out of Egypt by night. Sacrifice as the Passover to the LORD your God an animal from your flock or herd at the place the LORD will choose as a dwelling for his Name. Do not eat it with bread made with yeast, but for *seven days* eat unleavened bread, the bread of affliction, because you left Egypt in haste—so that all the days of your life you may remember the time of your departure from Egypt. Let no yeast be found in your possession in all your land for *seven days*. Do not let any of the meat you sacrifice on the *evening of the first day* remain until morning.

You must not sacrifice the Passover in any town the LORD your God gives you except in the place he will choose as a dwelling for his Name. There you must sacrifice the Passover *in the evening, when the sun goes down,* on the anniversary of your departure from Egypt [*Nisan 14*]. Roast it and eat it at the place the LORD your God will choose. Then in the morning return to your tents. For *six* [additional] days eat unleavened bread and on the *seventh* day hold an assembly to the Lord your God and do no work. (Deut. 16:1–8, italics added)

This is the first instance of including the Feast of Unleavened Bread in the Passover celebration. The fact that this was going to be the case was made clear when God gave the first Passover instructions to Moses back in Egypt.

The Feast of Unleavened Bread

This is a day you are to commemorate; for the generations to come you shall celebrate it as a festival to the LORD—a lasting ordinance. For *seven days* you are to eat bread made without yeast. On the first day remove the yeast from your houses, for whoever eats anything with yeast in it from the *first day* through the *seventh* must be cut off from Israel. On the *first* day hold a sacred assembly, and another one on the *seventh* day. Do no work at all on these days, except to prepare food for everyone to eat—that is all you may do.

Celebrate the Feast of Unleavened Bread, because it was on this very day that I brought your divisions out of Egypt. Celebrate this day as a lasting ordinance for the generations to come. In the first month you are to eat bread made without yeast, from the *evening of the fourteenth* day *until* the *evening of the twenty-first* day. For *seven* days no yeast is to be found in your houses. And whoever eats anything with yeast in it must be cut off from the community of Israel, whether he is an alien or native-born. Eat nothing made with yeast. Wherever you live, you must eat unleavened bread. (Exod. 12:14–20, italics added)

Appendix A—A History of the Passover

Moses Instructs the People

Then Moses said to the people, "Commemorate this day [Nisan 14], the day you came out of Egypt, out of the land of slavery, because the LORD brought you out of it with a mighty hand. Eat nothing containing yeast. Today, in the month of Abib [Nisan], you are leaving. When the LORD brings you into the land of the Canaanites, Hittites, Amorites, Hivites and Jebusites—the land he swore to your forefathers to give you, a land flowing with milk and honey—you are to observe this ceremony in this month: For *seven* days eat bread made without yeast and on the *seventh* day hold a festival to the LORD. Eat unleavened bread during those *seven days;* nothing with yeast in it is to be seen among you, nor shall any yeast be seen anywhere within your borders. On that day tell your son, 'I do this because of what the LORD did for me when I came out of Egypt.' This observance will be for you like a sign on your hand and a reminder on your forehead that the law of the LORD is to be on your lips. For the LORD brought you out of Egypt with his mighty hand. You must keep this ordinance at the appointed time year after year." (Exod. 13:3–10, italics added)

Points of Importance

The feast of unleavened bread was to be a six-day (Deut. 16:8) festival commencing on the *fifteenth* day of Nisan; the day after the celebration of the Passover. Together with the Passover on the *fourteenth*, this would make a *seven*-day period during which unleavened bread was to be eaten, beginning with twilight on the fourteenth and ending with twilight on the twenty-first. This seven-day period was to commence with a "sacred assembly" on the first day and conclude with a "sacred assembly" on the seventh day. The Passover was to commemorate the "passing over" of the houses of the Israelites on that night of death in Egypt; while the Feast of Unleavened Bread was a commemoration of the "bread of affliction" (Deut. 16:3), which was the unleavened bread they ate after leaving Egypt, due to the haste with which they left. The two together were to commemorate the deliverance of national Israel from the bondage in Egypt, and they were to keep the celebration year after year. The combination of these two celebrations into a single feast of seven days' duration is summarized in Leviticus twenty-three.

Prelude to Glory

These are the LORD's appointed feasts, the sacred assemblies you are to proclaim at their appointed times: The LORD's Passover begins at *twilight on the fourteenth* day of the first month. On the *fifteenth* day of that month the LORD's Feast of Unleavened Bread begins; for *seven* days you must eat bread made without yeast. On the first day [Nisan 14] hold a sacred assembly and do no regular work. For *seven* days present an offering made to the LORD by the fire. And on the *seventh* day [Nisan 20] hold a sacred assembly and do no regular work. (Lev. 23:4-8, italics added)

Thus, the manner in which this seven-day period was to be celebrated in the promised land was established. Additionally, a detailed description of the "offering made to the LORD by fire" is given in the book of Numbers.

On the *fourteenth day* of the first month the LORD's Passover is to be held. On the *fifteenth day* of this month there is to be a festival; for *seven days* eat bread made without yeast. On the first day hold a sacred assembly and do no regular work. Present to the LORD an offering made by fire, a burnt offering of two young bulls, one ram and seven male lambs a year old, all without defect. With each bull prepare a grain offering of three-tenths of an ephah of fine flour mixed with oil; with the ram, two-tenths; and with each of the seven lambs, one-tenth. Include one male goat as a sin offering to make atonement for you. Prepare these in addition to the regular morning burnt offering. In this way prepare the food for the offering made by fire every day for seven days as an aroma pleasing to the LORD; it is to be prepared in addition to the regular burnt offering and its drink offering. On the *seventh* day hold a sacred assembly and do no regular work. (Num. 28:16–25, italics added)

There was another two-part aspect to the celebration. The Passover meal was to be a family celebration. The lamb was to be killed by the men of the household, outside the environs of the camp, and the meal would be consumed in the same location. The next morning, they were to return to their tents and continue eating unleavened bread for the next six days. This was the family side of the celebration and was celebrated within the family context, even though only the men participated.

The other aspect of the celebration was the public participation which was conducted by the priests. These were the various

Appendix A—A History of the Passover

sacrifices made during the seven-day period on behalf of the people. This would be changed in Jesus' time but it is important to note here that the original Passover celebration as directed by God was entirely within the family context. Also it is important to notice that wine still was not a part of the celebration insofar as divine direction was concerned. This would also change in Jesus' time.

Hezekiah's Passover

The next Passover recorded in scripture was that of King Hezekiah which was celebrated in Jerusalem in approximately 720 B.C. Even though this was after the kingdom was divided into Israel and Judah, all were invited and some of the people from Israel came to Jerusalem to join in the celebration.

> Hezekiah sent word to all Israel and Judah and also wrote letters to Ephraim and Manasseh, inviting them to come to the temple of the LORD in Jerusalem and celebrate the Passover to the LORD, the God of Israel. The king and his officials and the whole assembly in Jerusalem decided to celebrate the Passover in the second month. They had not been able to celebrate it at the regular time because not enough priests had consecrated themselves and the people had not assembled in Jerusalem. The plan seemed right both to the king and to the whole assembly. They decided to send a proclamation throughout Israel, from Beersheba to Dan, calling the people to come to Jerusalem and celebrate the Passover to the LORD, the God of Israel. It had not been celebrated in large numbers according to what was written. (II Chron. 30:1–5)
>
> A very large crowd of people assembled in Jerusalem to celebrate the Feast of Unleavened Bread in the second month. They removed the altars in Jerusalem and cleared away the incense altars and threw them into the Kidron Valley.
>
> They slaughtered the Passover lamb on the fourteenth day of the second month. The priest and the Levites were ashamed and consecrated themselves and brought burnt offerings to the temple of the LORD. Then they took up their regular positions as prescribed in the Law of Moses the man of God. The priests sprinkled the blood handed to them by the Levites. Since many in the crowd had not consecrated themselves, the Levites had to kill the Passover lambs for all those who were not ceremonially clean and

Prelude to Glory

could not consecrate their lambs to the LORD. Although most of the many people who came from Ephraim, Manasseh, Issachar and Zebulun had not purified themselves, yet they ate the Passover, contrary to what was written. But Hezekiah prayed for them saying, "May the LORD, who is good, pardon everyone who sets his heart on seeking God—the LORD, the God of his fathers—even if he is not clean according to the rules of the sanctuary." And the LORD heard Hezekiah and healed the people.

The Israelites who were present in Jerusalem celebrated the Feast of Unleavened Bread for *seven* days with great rejoicing, while the Levites and priests sang to the LORD every day, accompanied by the LORD's instruments of praise.

Hezekiah spoke encouragingly to all the Levites, who showed good understanding of the service of the LORD. For the seven days they ate their assigned portion and offered fellowship offerings and praised the LORD, the God of their fathers. (II Chron. 30:13–22, italics added)

Points of Importance

This appears to be the first time the feast was celebrated in the temple at Jerusalem. For this reason many living outside the city refused to attend. The feast was held in the second month rather than the first for the reasons stated. Also, the Levites were given the job of killing the lambs for those who were unclean and the priests sprinkled the blood on the altar. Both of these actions appear to have been performed here for the first time. This also marks the first time since Joshua that the feast was celebrated on a national scale. There is no record as to whether or not some of the families had celebrated the Passover as a family event during the intervening years. However, God gave this celebration his approval and it did represent a step forward in restoring the ordinances of the Law of Moses. The Passover still would not be kept in full accordance with the ancient ordinances until the days of King Josiah, approximately 620 B.C.

Josiah's Passover

Josiah celebrated the Passover to the LORD in Jerusalem, and the Passover lamb was slaughtered on the *fourteenth* day of the first month. He appointed the priests to their duties and encouraged

Appendix A—A History of the Passover

them in the service of the LORD's temple. He said to the Levites, who instructed all Israel and who had been consecrated to the LORD: "Put the sacred ark in the temple that Solomon son of David king of Israel built. It is not to be carried about on your shoulders. Now serve the LORD your God and his people Israel. Prepare yourselves by families in your divisions, according to the directions written by David king of Israel and by his son Solomon.

"Stand in the holy place with a group of Levites for each subdivision of the families of your fellow countrymen, the lay people. Slaughter the Passover lambs, consecrate yourselves and prepare the lambs for your fellow countrymen, doing what the LORD commanded through Moses."

Josiah provided for all the lay people who were there a total of thirty thousand sheep and goats for the Passover offerings, and also three thousand cattle—all from the king's own possessions.

His officials also contributed voluntarily to the people and the priests and Levites. Hilkiah, Zechariah and Jehiel, the administrators of God's temple, gave the priests twenty-six hundred Passover offerings and three hundred cattle. Also Conaniah along with Shemaiah and Nethanel, his brothers, and Hashabiah, Jeiel and Jozabad, the leaders of the Levites, provided five thousand Passover offerings and five hundred head of cattle for the Levites.

The service was arranged and the priests stood in their places with the Levites in their divisions as the king had ordered. The Passover lambs were slaughtered, and the priests sprinkled the blood handed to them, while the Levites skinned the animals. They set aside the burnt offerings to give them to the subdivisions of the families of the people to offer to the LORD, as is written in the Book of Moses. They did the same with the cattle. They roasted the Passover animals over the fire as prescribed, and boiled the holy offerings in pots, cauldrons and pans and served them quickly to all the people. After this, they made preparations for themselves and for the priests, because the priests, the descendants of Aaron, were sacrificing the burnt offerings and the fat portions until nightfall. So the Levites made preparations for themselves and for the Aaronic priests.

The musicians, the descendants of Asaph, were in the places prescribed by David, Asaph, Heman and Jeduthun the king's seer. The gatekeepers at each gate did not need to leave their posts, because their fellow Levites made the preparations for them.

So at that time the entire service of the LORD was carried out for the celebration of the Passover and the offering of burnt offerings on the altar of the LORD, as King Josiah had ordered. The Israelites who were present celebrated the Passover at that time and observed the Feast of Unleavened Bread for seven days. The Passover had not been observed like this in Israel since the days of the prophet Samuel; and none of the kings of Israel had ever celebrated such a Passover as did Josiah, with the priests, the Levites and all Judah and Israel who were there with the people of Jerusalem. This Passover was celebrated in the eighteenth year of Josiah's reign. (II Chron. 35:1–19, italics added)

Points of Importance

This was the first time that a Passover of national magnitude had been celebrated since the time of Samuel. Prior to this celebration an ancient "book of law" had been discovered during the renovation of Solomon's temple (II Chron. 34:8ff; II Kings 22:3ff). This is believed by many to have been the book of Deuteronomy because of similarities between the two writings. Josiah had convened a solemn assembly at the temple for the public reading of the law and the renewal of the nation's covenant with Jehovah. The people began by purging Jerusalem from idolatry, then Bethel and other areas. It was evidently through the study of this lost book of the law that the ancient celebration of the Passover was rediscovered and instituted by Josiah.

This Passover, as described, was very similar to that form outlined to Moses at the time of Joshua. A few differences are worth noting. First, the sacrificing of the lambs was moved from the home to the temple. Second, the sacrifice was made by the Levites for *all* the people whereas before it was only for those people who were ceremonially unclean. But the meal was apparently still consumed in the home and within the family context. It seems, however, that the celebration was becoming more a national event held in the temple and less a family celebration, as the first Passovers were. The next Passover recorded in scripture would be celebrated under Ezra following the Israelites' return from the Babylonian captivity. Prior to that return, however, a vision was given to the prophet Ezekiel which must be inserted at this point.

Appendix A—A History of the Passover
Ezekiel's Vision

In approximately 572 B.C., while the nation of Israel was still in exile, Ezekiel was given a vision of the restored temple and holy days. Part of this vision concerned the celebration of the Passover and is important for showing the status of the Passover observance at that point in time. This regulations given Ezekiel in his vision were to be implemented when the nation of Israel returned from exile.

> In the first month on the *fourteenth day* you are to observe the *Passover, a feast lasting seven days,* during which you shall eat bread made without yeast. On that day the prince is to provide a bull as a sin offering for himself and for all the people of the land. Every day during the seven days of the Feast he is to provide seven bulls and seven rams without defect as a burnt offering to the LORD, and a male goat for a sin offering. He is to provide as a grain offering an ephah for each bull and an ephah for each ram, along with a hin of oil for each ephah. (Ezek. 45:21–24, italics added)

Points of Importance

By this time the Passover had been clearly established as a feast of seven days, beginning on the fourteenth, and lasting through the twentieth, during which only unleavened bread was to be eaten. Also, the name "Passover" was used to refer to the entire seven-day period.

Ezra's Passover

> On the fourteenth day of the first month, the exiles celebrated the Passover. The priests and Levites had purified themselves and were all ceremonially clean. The Levites slaughtered the Passover lamb for all the exiles, for their brothers the priests and for themselves. So the Israelites who had returned from the exile ate it, together with all who had separated themselves from the unclean practices of their Gentile neighbors in order to seek the LORD, the God of Israel. For seven days they celebrated with joy the Feast of Unleavened Bread, because the LORD had filled them with joy by changing the attitude of the king of Assyria, so that he assisted

Prelude to Glory

them in the work on the house of God, the God of Israel. (Ezra 6:19–22)

Points of Importance

This is the last record of a Passover celebrated in Old Testament times. By this point the custom of the Levites making the sacrifice for the people had become a fixed part of the ceremony. Also, the transition from a "family event" to a "temple celebration" had been completed. The record is silent as to whether these changes were of God or the result of rabbinic tradition.

Summary of Passover History

The Passover was the "passing over" of the houses of the Israelites who were living in Egypt at the time God took the lives of all the firstborn. God commanded that the night be commemorated by a feast held on the fourteenth of Nisan, the day of the Passover. The feast was to begin at the setting of the sun, which began the fourteenth of Nisan, with the sacrifice of a lamb. The lamb was then to be eaten, along with unleavened bread and bitter herbs in the same night. Any part of the lamb remaining in the morning was to be burned.

Celebration of the Passover was to commence the following year. Another celebration, the Feast of Unleavened Bread, which was to be a reminder of the hardship suffered in the exodus, was also commanded at that same time, but its commencement was postponed until Israel's arrival in the promised land.

The first commemoration of the Passover was celebrated at Sinai one year later on the first anniversary of the Passover. The meal was the same as that which had been eaten at the original Passover. The next recorded celebration of the Passover was that described in the book of Numbers which took place under Joshua immediately after entering the promised land. That celebration included the Feast of Unleavened Bread which commenced on the fifteenth of Nisan and lasted for six days. The two festivals were combined from that time forward and the seven-day period without leavened bread became commonly referred to as the

Appendix A—A History of the Passover

"Feast of Unleavened Bread," with the first day (Nisan 14) and the last day (Nisan 20) being days of holy convocation in which no work could be done except for the cooking of the food necessary for the feast.

This then was the status of the festival at the close of the Old Testament period. The nature of the festival had changed from what it was in the beginning, basically a family celebration, to one which required a priesthood and a temple. Part of this change was accepted by God, although the scriptures are silent as to whether or not all the changes were acceptable. In his book, *The Jewish Festivals*, Hayyim Schauss makes the following comments about these changes:

> It was in this way that the Pesach [Passover] and the Feast of Unleavened Bread were joined together, and two distinct spring festivals became one historical holiday, a symbol of the striving of the people toward national freedom. But since the festival was still bound up with the family, or, at most, the village community, it could not yet become a great national holiday. It was only later, when Pesach was observed by all Jews in one place, in one great sanctuary, that it gained national importance.
>
> This happened in the last few decades before the destruction of the first temple, in the time of Josiah, King of Judah. Israel, the great Jewish kingdom of the north, was no more. All that remained was Judah, the smaller kingdom of the south. In the reign of Josiah there was a strong progressive party, seeking to reconstruct Jewish national life and establish it on a new basis of justice and right. Sweeping reforms were instituted. One of the most outstanding was the elimination of all the "high places" because Jerusalem was declared the one sanctuary for all the Jews. Sacrifices were forbidden anywhere else and only Jerusalem was to be the goal of the pilgrimages made at holiday time. The festivals, therefore, lost their local character and became national observances that united all Jews in the one holy place, the Temple in Jerusalem.
>
> Through this reform, the Pesach ceremonial took on almost a new character. Since it was forbidden to make the Paschal sacrifice anywhere but in the Temple at Jersualem, it was impossible to smear the blood of the sacrificial lamb upon the doorpost of the house. In general, the observance lost its ancient weird character. The Book of Kings tells us truly that such a Pesach as was observed

in the eighteenth year of the reign of Josiah, the year in which the reform was instituted, had not been celebrated since the Jews settled in Palestine.

We cannot be certain how long a time passed before the Jews accepted these reforms in practice and ceased to offer the Pesach sacrifice in their own homes. Nor can we be certain how long it took for Pesach and the Feast of Unleavened Bread to become as one festival. But we do know that the importance of the festival grew and that it became the greatest Jewish national holiday. Sukkos remained the most festive and most joyous of the holidays, but Pesach attained the greatest national importance.

The highest point in the evolution of Pesach came in the last century of the second Temple, when the Jews suffered from the heavy oppression of the Romans. It was during this period that the Messianic hope flamed up, and in the minds of the Jews the deliverance of the future became bound up with the first redemption in Jewish history: the deliverance from Egypt. Jews had long believed that in the deliverance to come, God would show the same sort of miracles that he had performed in redeeming the Jews from Egypt. This belief gained added strength in this period of Roman occupation and oppression. Jews began to believe that the Messiah would be a second Moses and would free the Jews the self-same eve, the eve of Pesach. So Pesach became the festival of the second as well as the first redemption; in every part of the world where Jews lived, especially in Palestine, Jewish hearts beat faster on the eve of Pesach, beat with the hope that this night the Jews would be freed from the bondage of Rome, just as their ancestors were released from Egyptian slavery.

The ritual of the Pesach eve had, by that time, developed to rich proportions and was entirely different from the spring festival of the Jewish shepherds of old. The great Greco-Roman civilization ruled almost the entire known world and influenced the Jews to observe their holiday in a richer, more luxurious fashion. They adopted the wine and the soft sofas and the other luxuries that in those days were part of a feast. Jews still partook of the meat of the sacrificial lamb, but not in haste, as the Samaritan sect does to this very day; they ate leisurely and reclined on the softest of cushions.

The Pesach ritual at that time was a compromise between the Pesach of the very old days that was observed in the home, and the Pesach that followed it, the holiday that was observed only in the Temple. Observance, therefore, was divided into two main parts, and was celebrated in two different places, the Temple and

Appendix A—A History of the Passover

the home. In the afternoon of the day *before* Pesach, the sacrificial animal was slaughtered with elaborate ceremonies in the Temple; it was then taken home, roasted, and eaten in groups, with ceremonies that are almost identical with the Sedar observed by Jews today. Outside of Jerusalem the offering of sacrifices was not allowed and Pesach eve was observed in the home, in the family circle, and in the synagogue. In some places, however, it was customary to eat roast lamb, though no sacrifice was offered.

Passover in Jesus' Day

During the five-hundred-year period between the Jews' return from exile and the birth of Jesus, the nation made considerable changes which affected their relationship with God. They had divided themselves into sects that differed from one another in the manner in which they interpreted the scriptures and sought to carry them out. These differences resulted in changes in the Passover celebration and thus are important to this study.

First was the introduction of wine into the ceremony. No mention of wine is made in any of the Old Testament accounts of the Passover. This addition came strictly as a result of rabbinic teaching, such as:

> On the eve of Passover, from the close of the afternoon offering, one must not eat a thing until nightfall. Even the poorest in Israel then must not eat without reclining. And he must be allotted not less than *four glasses of wine*, even if these have to come from the charity kitchens. (Mish., Pes. 10.1, italics added).

The second change concerned work done on the fourteenth. As will be discussed shortly, the fourteenth was no longer considered a Sabbath; rather the fifteenth was made a Sabbath. Concerning work on the fourteenth, the Mishna states,

> Where the custom is to work on Passover eve until midday one may work until midday, but in a place where the custom is not to work, one must not work. If a man went from a place where the custom is not to work to a place where the custom is to work, or from a place where the custom is to work to a place where the

custom is not to work, he is bound by the stricter custom of the place whence he came, or to the stricter custom of the place to which he has come. But on no account must he act differently from the local custom, because it may lead to strife. (Mish., Pes. 4.1)

Even the practice of eating roast lamb on the Passover night became optional.

In a place where the practice was to eat roast meat on Passover night, one should eat roast meat; where the custom is not to eat, one must not eat it. (Mish., Pes. 4.4)

As indicated by the Mishnah, the manner of celebration depended on where in Palestine a person was when the Passover came. The country people in Galilee had a different celebration from the people who occupied Judea. Even the day of the celebration was different in Galilee and Judea. Those who wished to participate in the "temple celebration" had to come to Jerusalem, and they did so by the thousands. However, the Passover could be celebrated in other parts of Palestine without the sacrifice of a lamb.

The most flagrant and potentially confusing change in the Passover celebration had to do with the dates the festival was held. As has been clearly shown above, the Passover, as established by God, was to last *seven* days, beginning with the fourteenth of Nisan and continuing *through* the twentieth of Nisan, or *until* the twenty-first. The first and last days of this festival were to be holy days or Sabbaths (Lev. 23:4–8). The first day, the fourteenth, was the "Passover" and the seven-day period as a whole was referred to as the "Feast of Unleavened Bread," although Ezekiel does refer to the entire period as "Passover" (Ezek. 45:21). This was not the case, however, in the days of Jesus. The fourteenth continued to be the day the lamb was sacrificed, but the time of the sacrifice was moved from "just after sunset" forward to three the following afternoon.

The Testimony of Josephus

Regarding the time of the sacrifice, Josephus says:

Appendix A—A History of the Passover

So these high priests, upon the coming of their feast which is called the Passover, when they slay their sacrifices, *from the ninth hour to the eleventh,* [our 3:00 to 5:00 P.M.] but so that a company not less than ten belonging to each sacrifice . . . (Wars VI, IX, 3; italics added)

And as the feast of unleavened bread was at hand, in the first month, which according to the Macedonians, is called Xanthicus, but according to us Nisan, all the people ran together out of the villages to the city, and celebrated the festival, having purified themselves, with their wives and children, according to the law of their country; and they offered the sacrifice which was called the Passover, on the fourteenth day of the same month, and feasted seven days. (Ant. XI, IV, 8)

These two quotations clearly show that the lamb was sacrificed between 3:00 and 5:00 P.M., our time, on the fourteenth of Nisan.

A day was also added to the feast, thereby making it an eight-day feast rather than seven. Notice again what Josephus says.

In the month of Xanthicus, which is by us called Nisan, and is the beginning of our year, on the *fourteenth* day of the lunar month, when the sun is in Aries, (for in this month it was that we were delivered from bondage under the Egyptians), the law ordained that we should every year slay that sacrifice which I before told you we slew when we came out of Egypt, and which is called the *Passover;* and so do we celebrate this Passover in companies, leaving nothing of what we sacrifice till the day following. *The feast of unleavened bread succeeds that of the Passover,* and falls on the *fifteenth* day of the month, and *continues seven days,* wherein they feed on unleavened bread. (Ant. III, X, 5; italics added)

. . . for what they brought with them out of Egypt would not suffice them any longer time; and only while they dispensed it to each person, to use so much only as would serve for necessity, but not for satiety. Whence it is that, in memory of the want we were then in, we keep a feast for *eight days,* which is called the *Feast of Unleavened Bread.* (Ant. II, XV, 1; italics added)

Thus, in Jesus' time, the Passover lamb was slaughtered late in the afternoon of the fourteenth, but not eaten until after sundown which was, according to Jewish time, the fifteenth of Nisan. The eating of the meal had been moved forward twenty-four hours. The fifteenth was made the first day of the Feast of Unleavened Bread, and the twenty-first was made the seventh day. Therefore, the *fifteenth* and *twenty-first* days were made Sabbaths rather than the fourteenth and twentieth as God had originally directed. The day *after* the Passover became a Sabbath rather than the day *of* the Passover. This change, incidentally, was never accepted by the Essenes who had a colony in western Jerusalem; nor was it accepted in the rural areas of Galilee, both of which continued to observe the festival in the ancient manner.

The last change in the Passover celebration worth noting was in who was invited to the Passover meal. Originally the Passover had been a family festival celebrated within the context of the biological family. Only when necessary to make the required group of ten was a second family invited to join the celebration. By Jesus' day, however, it became customary to make a large banquet of the affair and invite upwards of fifty or a hundred guests. Being invited to celebrate the Passover in the home of the more influential became a status symbol and, when invited, one would wear his finest in clothing and jewelry. One lamb could no longer feed the guests at these celebrations; so two, three, and if necessary, more lambs were added. These additional lambs were called the Chagigah. They were a voluntary peace offering made by private individuals. The breast was given to the priests as a wave offering and the right shoulder as a heave offering. What remained of the lamb might be eaten by the offerer and his guest on the day on which it was slain or on the second day, but if any portion was left until the third day it was burned.

Conclusion

The Passover celebration had originally been established by God to commemorate the night he passed over the homes of the Israelites and took the lives of the firstborn of Egypt. The celebration was to be marked by sacrificing and eating a lamb between the sunset and midnight that began the fourteenth of Nisan. It was to be conducted entirely within the family context.

Upon entering the promised land, a six-day feast called the

Appendix A—A History of the Passover

Feast of Unleavened Bread was added to the celebration. This feast was to begin on the fifteenth of Nisan and continue through the twentieth. From the fourteenth through the twentieth of Nisan no leavened bread was even permitted in the home. In time, the names "Passover" and "Feast of Unleavened Bread" came to be used interchangeably.

During the next fifteen hundred years numerous changes were made in the celebration. Some, but certainly not all, of the changes made during the Old Testament period appear to have been approved by God. By the time of the New Testament the celebration had been entirely restructured and was being celebrated in a manner totally different from the original instructions.

The sacrifice of the lamb had been moved from just after sunset to three o'clock the following afternoon. The requirement was added that the lambs be sacrificed in the temple in Jerusalem. Eating the lamb was moved 24 hours to just after the sunset that began on the fifteenth of Nisan. Wine was added to the feast and the local character of the event gave way to a national observance that united all Jews in the temple in Jerusalem. A day was added to the celebration which made it an eight-day feast.

These changes were accepted by the rulers, but there was a large minority group that refused to accept them. The Essenes and many of the rural people of Galilee continued to celebrate the event in accordance with the ancient commandments. Thus, when Jesus arrived in Jerusalem to celebrate the Passover he found a situation totally different from what one would visualize from reading the Old Testament instructions.

APPENDIX B

Timetable

By applying certain estimates and assumptions it is possible to produce a timetable which will help place the events surrounding Jesus' death, burial, and resurrection in some perspective. This, however, should be approached with extreme caution, for two thousand years have obliterated the evidence necessary to reconstruct the exact times involved. The following table is highly subjective. The estimates and assumptions used to construct it are detailed at the end of the table.

Wednesday, Nisan 13. A.D. 30

4:00 P.M. Jesus and the disciples arrive outside Jerusalem.
Peter and John are sent into the city to prepare the Passover meal.

Thursday, Nisan 14, A.D. 30

6:00 P.M. *Peter and John prepare the Passover meal at the house of John Mark.
8:00 P.M. Jesus eats the Passover meal with the disciples.
9:00 P.M. Jesus sends Judas out.
9:20 P.M. Judas arrives at the temple.
9:40 P.M. Judas departs the temple.
10:00 P.M. Judas arrives at the house of the high priest.
Jesus and his disciples leave Mark's house.
10:10 P.M. Judas departs the house of the high priest.
10:20 P.M. Judas arrives at Annas' house.
10:30 P.M. Jesus and the disciples arrive at the Garden of Gethsemane.

Appendix B—Timetable

	Judas departs Annas' house.
10:50 p.m.	Judas arrives at the fortress of Antonia.
11:20 p.m.	Judas departs the fortress of Antonia.
11:40 p.m.	Judas arrives at Mark's house.
11:45 p.m.	Judas departs Mark's house.
12:15 a.m.	Judas arrives at Gethsemane with the soldiers.
12:30 a.m.	The soldiers lead Jesus from the Garden of Gethsemane.
1:00 a.m.	Jesus is taken before Annas.
1:30 a.m.	Jesus is taken to the palace of the high priest.
3:30 a.m.	Peter and John arrive at the palace of the high priest. Peter denies Jesus for the first time.
4:00 a.m.	Peter denies Jesus for the second time.
4:30 a.m.	Jesus is tried by Caiaphas.
5:00 a.m.	Jesus departs the house of Caiaphas.
5:00 a.m.	Peter denies Jesus for the third time. The cock crows.
5:30 a.m.	*Jesus is tried by the Sanhedrin.
6:00 a.m.	*Jesus is tried by Pilate.
6:40 a.m.	Jesus is tried by Herod.
7:10 a.m.	Jesus is tried by Pilate a second time.
7:30 a.m.	The Roman soldiers scourge Jesus.
8:00 a.m.	Jesus is sentenced.
8:30 a.m.	Jesus departs for Golgotha.
8:50 a.m.	Jesus arrives at Golgotha.
9:00 a.m.	*Jesus is placed on the cross.
12:00 p.m.*	Darkness covers the land.
3:00 p.m.	*The Jewish sacrifice of Passover lambs begins at the temple.
3:00 p.m.	*Jesus dies on the cross.
	*An earthquake.
	*The temple veil is destroyed.

Prelude to Glory

  4:00 P.M.   Joseph of Arimathea asks Pilate for Jesus' body.
  4:30 P.M.   Jesus' body is removed from the cross.
  5:45 P.M. *The body is placed in the tomb.

Friday, Nisan 15, A.D. 30

  6:00 P.M. *Passover Sabbath begins.
  6:30 P.M.   The Jewish authorities ask that the tomb be sealed.
  7:00 P.M.   The tomb is sealed and a Roman guard set.

Saturday, Nisan 16, A.D. 30

  6:00 P.M. *The seventh-day Sabbath begins.
  5:00 P.M. *Mary Magdalene and the other Mary visit the tomb.

Sunday, Nisan 17, A.D. 30

  6:00 P.M. *The seventh-day Sabbath ends.
  6:30 P.M. *The two Marys and Salome purchase spices.
  7:30 P.M.   The women prepared the spices to anoint the body.
  6:30 A.M.   Mary Magdalene; Mary, the mother of James; and Salome depart John's house for the tomb.
  6:50 A.M.   The three women arrive at the tomb.
  6:55 A.M.   Mary Magdalene returns to get Peter and John.
  7:05 A.M.   The other Mary and Salome speak with the angels.
  7:10 A.M.   The two women depart for Mark's house.
  7:15 A.M.   Mary Magdalene arrives at John's house.
  7:20 A.M.   Peter and John leave for the tomb.
  7:30 A.M.   Mary and Salome arrive at Mark's house.
  7:40 A.M.   Peter and John arrive at the tomb.
  7:45 A.M.   Peter and John depart from the tomb.
  7:50 A.M.   Mary Magdalene talks with the angels and Jesus.
  8:00 A.M.   Mary Magdalene departs from the tomb.
  8:10 A.M.   The women depart Mark's for John's house.

Appendix B—Timetable

	The delegation departs Mark's house for the tomb.
	The soldiers report to the Jewish authorities.
8:15 A.M.	The women meet Jesus en route to John's house.
8:20 A.M.	Mary Magdalene and the other women arrive at John's house.
8:25 A.M.	Peter departs for the tomb a second time.
	The delegation from Mark's house arrives at the tomb.
8:30 A.M.	The delegation departs from the tomb.
8:45 A.M.	Peter arrives at the tomb for the second time.
8:50 A.M.	Peter departs from the tomb.
	The delegation returns to Mark's house.
9:10 A.M.	Peter arrives at John's house.
1:30 P.M.	Two disciples depart Jerusalem for Emmaus.
2:00 P.M.	Jesus joins them en route.
4:30 P.M.	The three arrive at Emmaus.
4:50 P.M.	They recognize Jesus during the meal.
5:00 P.M.	The disciples depart Emmaus to return to Jerusalem.
7:30 P.M.	The apostles eat behind locked doors.
8:00 P.M.	The two from Emmaus report to the apostles.
8:10 P.M.	Jesus appears to the apostles—Thomas is absent.

*Time fixed by scripture or Jewish law.

The above table is highly speculative and should only be used to get a general time-frame for the events listed.

Estimates and Assumptions

1. The area within the walls of the city of Jerusalem in Jesus' day was estimated to be less than one square mile.
2. We know for a fact that the tomb was outside the walls (Heb. 13:12).
3. The tomb is believed to have been north of the city, while

the location of the upper room (Mark's house) is believed to have been in the southwest section of the upper city.
4. The houses of Annas and Caiaphas and Herod's palace are known to have also been in the southwest section of the upper city.
5. The temple and the fortress of Antonia were located in the northeast section of the city.
6. The Garden of Gethsemane is located partway up the Mount of Olives which is across the Kidron Valley.
7. John's house is also assumed to have been in the southwestern section of the city.

The estimates of time required to travel from one location to another used in the timetable are as follows:

Bethany gate to upper room	20 minutes
Upper room to temple	20 minutes
Temple to Caiaphas' house	20 minutes
Caiaphas' house to Annas' house	10 minutes
Annas' house to fortress of Antonia	20 minutes
Fortress of Antonia to upper room	20 minutes
Upper room to Gethsemane	30 minutes
Gethsemane to Annas' house	30 minutes
Caiaphas' house to Temple	20 minutes
Temple to fortress of Antonia	5 minutes
Fortress of Antonia to Herod's palace	20 minutes
Fortress of Antonia to Golgotha	20 minutes
John's house to garden tomb	20 minutes
Mark's house to garden tomb	20 minutes
John's house to Mark's house	10 minutes
Jerusalem to Emmaus	3 hours

APPENDIX C

The Day of Jesus' Crucifixion

Numerous scholars have expended considerable time and effort attempting to determine the day of the week on which Jesus was crucified. The Roman church accepted Friday as the correct day and inaugurated the celebration of Good Friday to commemorate the event. This decision was based on the fact that the day following Jesus' crucifixion was a Sabbath, a fact established by scripture (Mark 15:42; John 19:31); therefore, it has long been believed that the crucifixion had to be on a Friday. There is, however, a problem with sustaining a Friday crucifixion. Since there is no question that Jesus rose from the dead "early on the first day of the week," it is not possible to place "three days and three nights" (Matt. 12:40) between late Friday afternoon and early Sunday morning. This has been the source of the controversy.

Numerous arguments have been offered to show that the "wording" must be taken at something other than its face value. Perhaps the most common explanation of this type is that any portion of a given twenty-four hour period can be referred to as a "day and a night." Thus, it is argued that "part of Friday, all of Saturday, and part of Sunday" qualify as three days and three nights. Several variations of this explanation have been put forward but all fall short of convincing the skeptic.

The basic fallacy underlying this approach is the assumption that "Sabbath" always refers to the *seventh* day of the week, or our Saturday. To solve the mystery, it is necessary to begin with a study of Jewish Sabbath observances, both as commanded in the Old Testament and as observed during the first century.

Prelude to Glory
Jewish Sabbath Observances

Old Testament scripture makes it clear that there were "Sabbaths" other than the "seventh-day Sabbath." Notice the following:

> The LORD said to Moses, "Speak to the Israelites and say to them: 'These are my appointed feasts, the appointed feasts of the LORD, which you are to proclaim as *sacred assemblies* [holy convocations]. There are six days when you may work, but the seventh day is a Sabbath of rest, a day of sacred assembly. You are not to do any work; wherever you live, it is a Sabbath to the LORD.'" (Lev. 23:1–3, italics added)

This is clearly the seventh-day Sabbath with which the Old Testament student is very familiar. It is characterized by two main requirements, a day of rest and a day of sacred assembly. Continue reading and notice that other "Sabbaths" are also commanded.

> "These are the LORD's appointed feasts, the *sacred assemblies* you are to proclaim at their appointed times: The LORD's Passover begins at twilight on the fourteenth day of the first month. On the fifteenth day of that month the LORD's Feast of Unleavened Bread begins; for seven days you must eat bread made without yeast. On the first day [Passover] hold a *sacred assembly* [holy convocation] and do no regular work. For seven days present an offering made to the LORD by fire. And on the seventh day hold a sacred assembly and do no regular work." (Lev. 23:4–8, italics added)

This clearly shows that God intended for certain days other than the seventh day of the week to be observed as Sabbaths. That the Passover was one such day is further supported by the following scripture regarding the Feast of Unleavened Bread:

> On the first day [Passover] hold a sacred assembly, and another one on the seventh day. Do no work at all on these days, except to prepare food for everyone to eat—that is all you may do. (Exod. 12:16).

Appendix C—The Day of Jesus' Crucifixion

God commanded that Passover be observed as a Sabbath just like the seventh day of the week with the single exception that food could be prepared on the Passover Sabbath, whereas it could not be prepared on the seventh-day sabbath. This difference has a direct bearing on the subject being discussed. For reasons already discussed (see Appendix A), the Jews in the first century celebrated the Passover Sabbath on the fifteenth of Nisan.

It has also been shown (see Chapter Two, "The Day Jesus Celebrated the Passover") that Jesus was crucified on the fourteenth of Nisan. Therefore, the day following Jesus' crucifixion would have been a Sabbath regardless of the day of the week. In view of the scriptures cited, it becomes obvious that the day of the week on which Jesus was crucified cannot be determined by the fact that the next day was a Sabbath.

While it is impossible to establish with absolute certainty the day of the week on which Jesus was crucified, there are scriptures which indirectly bear on that day. A consideration of these scriptures will be valuable in helping the student determine where the weight of evidence lies.

The First-day Resurrection

The Gospel writers established beyond any doubt that Jesus was resurrected on the first day of the week.

Matt. 28:1 After the Sabbath, at dawn on the first day of the week, Mary Magdalene and the other Mary went to look at the tomb.

Mark 16:2 Very early on the first day of the week, just after sunrise, they were on their way to the tomb.

Luke 24:1 On the first day of the week, very early in the morning, the women took the spices they had prepared and went to the tomb.

John 20:1 Early on the first day of the week, while it was still dark, Mary of Magdala went to the tomb and saw that the stone had been removed from the entrance.

Prelude to Glory

It is commonly believed that John, who wrote his Gospel at the end of the first century, used Roman time in placing events while the synoptics, particularly Mark, used Jewish time (see Chapter Six, "The Time of the Crucifixion"). Since both John and the synoptics place the resurrection on the first day of the week, it is possible to narrow the time down to that period which would be considered the first day of the week under both systems. The Jewish system used a day which began and ended with sunset. The Roman day began and ended at midnight. The Jewish day began approximately six hours before the Roman day. Therefore, the time which was common to the first day in both systems was from midnight to sunset, a period of approximately eighteen hours. This places Jesus' resurrection during this period of time.

The period can be further shortened by considering the fact that the resurrection took place early in the morning before sunrise. This leaves a span of approximately six hours on the first day of the week during which the resurrection could have taken place. The scriptures clearly state that Jesus would be resurrected on the third day. If we begin with Sunday and count backward three days, we arrive at Thursday as being the day of the crucifixion.

There are eleven scriptures in the Gospels which state that Jesus would be resurrected on the third day.

Matthew 16:21; 17:23; 20:19; 27:63
Mark 9:31; 10:34
Luke 9:22; 13:32; 18:33; 24:7; 24:21

The last of these, Luke 24:21, states that the day of the resurrection was the third day. The third day in the tomb would begin with the forty-ninth hour.

Jesus died at the ninth hour or approximately three o'clock in the afternoon according to our time. He was placed in the tomb just prior to sunset. Considering the time necessary to obtain the body and prepare it for burial, it would be very difficult to assume that the burial took place any more than an hour before sunset. This leave a maximum of about one hour that the body could have been in the ground on the day of burial. Depending on whether one accepts a crucifixion day of Thursday or Friday, the actual hours Jesus spent in the tomb could be calculated as follows:

Appendix C—The Day of Jesus' Crucifixion
Hours in The Tomb

	Thursday Burial	Friday Burial
Thursday	1 hour	- - -
Friday	24 hours	1 hour
Saturday	24 hours	24 hours
Sunday	6–12 hours	6–12 hours
Total	55–61 hours	31–37 hours

This calculation clearly shows that a Friday burial would only allow Jesus to be in the tomb a maximum of thirty-seven hours which would not even be two full days. A Thursday burial, however, would place Jesus in the tomb between fifty-five and sixty-one hours. This would definitely place the resurrection on the third day.

The hours in the tomb alone indicate a Thursday crucifixion.

Three Days and Three Nights

Matt. 12:40   For as Jonah was three days and three nights in the belly of a huge fish, so the Son of Man will be three days and three nights in the heart of the earth.

While neither method of calculation places Jesus in the tomb for a full seventy-two hour period, a Thursday burial comes much closer to covering a period of three days and three nights. If part of a day can be considered a day and part of a night can be considered a night, then three days and three nights can easily be reconciled with a Thursday burial. There is no way, however, of reconciling three days and three nights with a Friday burial.

If, as has been shown, the Romans viewed the day as a twenty-four-hour period and the Jews viewed the day as a twelve-hour period and the night as a separate period (John 11:9–10), then Matthew, writing for the Jews, could say that Jesus would be in the tomb during three days and three nights. Again, we find that Thursday to Sunday in the tomb can be reconciled with that statement while Friday to Sunday cannot.

Prelude to Glory
The Day of Pentecost

Another indirect indicator of the day of the crucifixion is the day of Pentecost. Christian tradition has held that the day of Pentecost was a Sunday. There is no means of establishing the accuracy of this tradition. Even so, some very interesting points can be examined which also point more to a Thursday crucifixion than a Friday crucifixion.

There were two separate methods of calculating the day of Pentecost. The first was the method given by God for calculating the day for celebrating the Feast of Weeks. The other was the method used in the first century for calculating the day for celebrating the Feast of Pentecost. This difference has a bearing on the date of the Pentecost celebration during the first century. During Old Testament times this feast was always celebrated on the first day of the week. As will be seen, that was changed prior to the time of Jesus.

The Feast of Weeks

The Harvest Feast or Feast of Weeks can be viewed as a supplement to the Passover. This feast was originally a feast commemorating harvest held fifty days after the first Sabbath following the day the first sheaf of grain was cut.

> The LORD said to Moses, "Speak to the Israelites and say to them: 'When you enter the land I am going to give you and you reap its harvest, bring to the priest a sheaf of the first grain you harvest. He is to wave the sheaf before the LORD so it will be accepted on your behalf; the priest is to wave it on the day *after the Sabbath*. . . .
>
> From the day after the Sabbath, the day you brought the sheaf of the wave offering, count off seven full weeks. Count off fifty days up to the day after the seventh Sabbath, and then present an offering of new grain to the LORD.'" (Lev. 23:9–11, 15–23; italics added)

The date of the feast, therefore, would vary from year to year depending on whether the harvest was early or late, but it would

Appendix C—The Day of Jesus' Crucifixion

always fall on a Sunday. Long before New Testament times, however, the Jews began to regard this feast as a commemoration of the giving of the law on Mount Sinai, which occurred approximately fifty days after the Passover in Egypt. Not only was its meaning changed without divine authorization, but the date of the feast was made uniform from year to year by setting it fifty days after the Passover Feast and the name was changed from the Feast of Weeks to the Feast of the Pentecost.

The Pentecost

In Jesus' day Pentecost was dated from the Passover Sabbath rather than the seventh-day Sabbath. Because of this method of dating, Pentecost would fall on different days of the week depending on the day on which the Passover Sabbath fell. The Passover Sabbath always fell on the fifteenth day of Nisan. On the next day, the sixteenth of Nisan, the people brought sheaves of barley to the temple to be presented as a "wave offering." It was so called because the priest would wave the sheaves before the altar as an offering to God. This was done to satisfy the requirements of Leviticus 23:10. From the sixteenth of Nisan they would count fifty days which caused the Feast of Pentecost to always fall on the sixth day of Sivan, just as it does today.

Josephus makes the following statement concerning the dating of the Feast of Pentecost during the first century:

> But on the second day of unleavened bread, which is the sixteenth day of the month [Nisan], they first partake of the fruits of the earth, for before that day they do not touch them. And while they suppose it proper to honour God, from whom they obtain this plentiful provision in the first place, they offer the first-fruits of their barley, and that in the manner following: They take a handful of the ears, and dry them, then beat them small and purge the barley from the bran; they then bring one tenth deal to the altar, to God: and, casting one handful of it upon the fire, they leave the rest for the use of the priest; and after this it is that they may publicly or privately reap their harvest. They also at this participation of first-fruits of the earth, sacrifice a lamb, as a burnt offering to God.

> When a week of weeks has passed over after this sacrifice (which weeks contain forty and nine days), on the fiftieth day, which is Pentecost, but is called by the Hebrews Asartha, which signifies Pentecost, they bring to God a loaf, made of wheat flour, of two tenth deals, with leaven; and for sacrifices, they bring two lambs. (Ant. III, X, 5–6)

That the method used to calculate the date and day of Pentecost was changed between Exodus and the first century is further confirmed by the following statement from the Mishnah which shows that during the first century Pentecost fell on different days from year to year.

> If the Feast of Pentecost fell on the eve of a Sabbath, the School of Shammai say: The day for slaughtering is after the Sabbath. And the School of Hilles say: It needs no other day for slaughtering. But they agree that if [the Feast] fell on a Sabbath, the day for slaughtering is after the Sabbath. The High Priest may not put on his High-Priestly vestments, and mourning and fasting are permitted, to lend no support to the words of them that say, "Pentecost falls on the day after the Sabbath." (Mish., Hag. 2.4)

The last part of this statement refers to the Sadducees, who maintained that Pentecost must always fall on the first day of the week because of Leviticus 23. They took "Sabbath" literally, and not, as the Pharisees, in the sense of the first festival-day of Passover.

During the first century the Feast of Pentecost actually fell on the fifty-first day following the Feast of the Passover. It has been previously shown that Jesus was crucified on the day on which the Passover lamb was slaughtered which was the day before the Jews ate the Passover. Pentecost, therefore, fell on the fifty-second day following the day Jesus was crucified. If Jesus was crucified on Friday then Pentecost fell on Monday. If however, Jesus was crucified on Thursday, Pentecost would have fallen on Sunday.

It is up to each individual to decide how much credence to place in the tradition that Peter preached the first Gospel sermon on a Sunday and thereby set the precedent for the church meeting on the first day of the week. If one wishes to maintain that position, however, then he is forced to accept a Thursday crucifixion.

Appendix C—The Day of Jesus' Crucifixion
John's High Sabbath

John refers to the Sabbath following Jesus' crucifixion as a "high Sabbath" (John 19:31). There has been considerable discussion as to the exact meaning of a high Sabbath, with basically three resulting explanations.

One explanation is that "high Sabbath" merely refers to the fact that it was the Sabbath of a feast week. There is no scriptural support for this position and it seems highly unlikely that John would have made a special point of a fact as common and as obvious as that.

The second explanation is that this Sabbath day was both a seventh-day Sabbath and a Passover Sabbath. This explanation is necessary to maintain a Friday crucifixion but otherwise it has no merit. Again this would be making a special point of an obvious fact.

The third explanation is that "high Sabbath" was a term used to designate a forty-eight-hour Sabbath. This would be the case if the Passover Sabbath fell on a Friday. John is believed to have written his Gospel late in the first century to Romans who would not be familiar with the various Jewish festivals and the details surrounding each of them. Like people today, the Gentile world was familiar with the Jews' seventh-day Sabbath but few would have been familiar with the Passover Sabbath or the occasional forty-eight-hour Sabbaths when a special Sabbath fell back to back with a seventh-day Sabbath. This, some argue, is the reason John pointed out that this Sabbath was something other than the seventh-day Sabbath with which people were familiar.

It is impossible to know for sure if one of these three explanations is correct or if there was some other reason for John's making this point. Whatever the case, John seems to have felt that the fact needed to be pointed out that this Sabbath was not the ordinary seventh-day Sabbath.

The Missing Wednesday

The week in which Jesus was crucified was exceptionally busy. Every day is described in detail by the writers much more so than any other similar period in the Gospels. It is, therefore, difficult to understand why no mention is made of any activity on what has long been considered to be Wednesday of that week.

Some have stated that this was a day of rest preceeding the ordeal which began with the last supper and culminated with Jesus' death. This is merely speculation inasmuch as those maintaining this position are arguing from silence.

If, however, Jesus was crucified on Thursday then there would be no missing day. It has been the assumption of a Friday crucifixion that has caused the speculation concerning Wednesday.

The Day of Preparation

Mark, Luke, and John all state that Jesus was crucified on the "day of preparation." Some have argued that the "day of preparation" referred to Friday because that is the day on which the Jewish nation prepared for the Sabbath. It is true there were rules for Friday conduct designed to prepare for the seventh-day Sabbath. There is no evidence, however, that shows that this was a term universally applied to Friday by the Jewish nation. On the other hand, John 19:14 clearly states that it was "the preparation of the Passover." This terminology is commonly found in Jewish writings referring to the fourteenth of Nisan.

Conclusion

The above arguments all favor a Thursday crucifixion and burial. Other than the "subsequent Sabbath" argument, there is virtually nothing aside from tradition to support a Friday crucifixion. In view of this, my position is that the vast weight of evidence points to a Thursday crucifixion and burial.

BIBLIOGRAPHY

Alexander, David. *Eerdman's Handbook to the Bible*. Grand Rapids, Mich.: Eerdmans, 1973.

The Analytical Greek Lexicon. Grand Rapids, Mich.: Zondervan, 1970.

Arndt and Gingrich. *A Greek-English Lexicon of the New Testament*. Chicago: Univ. of Chicago Press, 1957.

Atlas of the Bible. Pleasantville, N.Y.: Readers Digest, 1981.

Auerbach, Leo. *The Babylonian Talmud in Selection*. New York: Philosophical Lib., 1944.

Barry, George R. *The Interlinear Literal Translation of the Hebrew Old Testament*. Grand Rapids, Mich.: Kregel, 1970.

Blaiklock, E. M. and R. K. Harrison. *Dictionary of Bible Archaeology*. Grand Rapids, Mich.: Regency Reference Library, 1983.

Block, Abraham. *The Biblical and Historical Background of the Jewish Holy Days*. New York: Ktav, 1978.

Bruce, A. B. *The Training of the Twelve*. Grand Rapids, Mich.: Kregel, 1971.

Coleman, William L. *Today's Handbook of Bible Times and Customs*. Minneapolis: Bethany, 1984.

Danby, Herbert, D. D. *The Mishnah (Translated from the Hebrew with Introduction and Brief Explanatory Notes)*. New York: Oxford Univ. Press, 1933.

Davies, A. Powell. *The Meaning of the Dead Sea Scrolls*. New York: Mentor Books, 1956.

Dehoff, George W. *Alleged Bible Contradictions Explained*. Murfreesboro, Tenn.: Dehoff Publications, 1962.

Easton, M. G. *Illustrated Bible Dictionary*. Eugene, Oreg.: Harvest House, 1978.

Edersheim, Alfred. *The Life and Times of Jesus the Messiah*. Grand Rapids, Mich.: Eerdmans, 1969.

———. *Sketches of Jewish Social Life in the Days of Christ*. Grand Rapids, Mich.: Eerdmans, 1972.

———. *The Temple—Its Ministry and Service*. Grand Rapids, Mich.: Eerdmans, 1969.

The Englishman's Greek Concordance of the New Testament. Grand Rapids, Mich.: Zondervan, 1970.

Fahling, Adam. *The Life of Christ*. St. Louis: Concordia, 1936.

Fausset, A. R. *Fausset's Bible Dictionary*. Grand Rapids, Mich.: Zondervan, 1967.

Ferguson, Everett. *Early Christians Speak*. Austin, Tex.: Sweet Publishing Co., 1971.

Freeman, James M. *Manners and Customs of the Bible*. Plainfield, N.J.: Logos, 1978.

Great People of the Bible and How They Lived. Pleasantville, N.Y.: Readers Digest, 1974.

Hendriksen, William. *Survey of the Bible*. Grand Rapids, Mich.: Baker, 1976.

Hester, H. I. *The Heart of Hebrew History*. Liberty, Mo.: Quality Press, 1962.

The Holy Bible—New International Version. Grand Rapids, Mich.: Zondervan, 1978.

Hort, Fenton John Anthony. *Judaistic Christianity*. Grand Rapids, Mich.: Baker, 1980.

House, H. Wayne. *Chronological and Background Charts of the New Testament*. Grand Rapids, Mich.: Zondervan, 1982.

The Interpreter's Bible. New York: Abingdon, 1952.

Jeremias, Joachim. *The Eucharistic Words of Jesus*. Philadelphia: Fortress Press, 1966.

Lauterbach, Jacob Z. *Mekilta De-Rabbi Ishmael*. Philadelphia: Jewish Pub. Society, 1933.

McBirnie, William S. *The Search for the Tomb of Jesus*. Montrose, Calif.: Acclaimed Books, 1975.

———*The Search for the Twelve Apostles*. Wheaton, Ill.: Tyndale, 1975.

Macknight, James. *A Harmony of the Four Gospels*. Grand Rapids, Mich.: Baker, 1950.

Margolis, Max L. and Alexander Marx. *A History of the Jewish People*. Chicago: Jewish Pub. Society, 1927.

Markve, Arthur. *A New Harmony of the Gospels*. Minneapolis: Bethany, 1957.

Marshall, Alfred. *The R.S.V. Interlinear Greek-English New Testament*. Grand Rapids, Mich.: Zondervan, 1958.

Moore, George F. *Judaism in the First Centuries of the Christian Era*. Cambridge, Mass.: Harvard Univ. Press, 1950.

The New Analytical Bible—Authorized Version. Chicago: John A. Dixon, 1950.

Ritchie, John. *Feasts of Jehovah*. Grand Rapids, Mich.: Kregel, 1982.

Robertson, A. T. *A Harmony of the Gospels for Students of the Life of Christ*. New York: Harper and Row, 1950.

Schauss, Hayyim. *Guide to Jewish Holy Days, (from Their Beginnings to Our Own Day)*. New York: Schockin Books, 1938.

———. *The Jewish Festivals*. U.S.A.: Union of American Hebrew Congregations, 1938.

Schurer, Emil. *A History of the Jewish People in the Time of Jesus*. New York: Schocken Books, 1961.

Smith, F. LaGard. *The Narrated Bible*. Eugene, Oreg.: Harvest House, 1984.

Bibliography

Smith, William. *The New Smith's Bible Dictionary*. Garden City, N.Y.: Doubleday, 1966.

———. *Old Testament History*. Joplin, Mo.: College Press, 1970.

Thayer, Joseph H. *Greek-English Lexicon of the New Testament*. Grand Rapids, Mich.: Zondervan, 1962.

Thompson, J. A. *The Bible and Archaeology*. Grand Rapids, Mich.: Eerdmans, 1957.

Unger, Merrill F. *The New Unger's Bible Handbook*. Chicago: Moody, 1984.

Vainstein, Yaaccy. *The Cycle of the Jewish Year*. Jerusalem,: The Department for Torah Education and Culture in the Disapora, The World Zionist Organization.

Walton, John H. *Chronological Charts of the Old Testament*. Grand Rapids, Mich.: Zondervan, 1952.

Whitson, William. *Josephus Complete Works*. Grand Rapids, Mich.: Kregel, 1960.

Wright, Fred H. *Manners and Customs of Bible Lands*. Chicago: Moody, 1953.

Young, Robert. *Analytical Concordance to the Bible*. Funk and Wagnall.

Zeitlin, Solomon. *The Rise and Fall of the Judaean State*. Philadelphia: Jewish Pub. Society, 1967.